"I love this book. Whether you need to redecorate, remodel, or totally renovate your life, Felicia has the tools you need to get the job done. Unlike other numerology books, this book compiles basic numerology information plus it goes a step further so you can identify strengths and weaknesses, and make positive changes in your life. It is simple, effective, full of examples and anecdotes, and delightful to read. I had so much fun reading it, doing the survey, and figuring out my own stuff... I couldn't put it down."

—JODY HOWARD, author of *A Soul's Guide to Abundance,*
Health, and Happiness

"Felicia takes a playful, fun, and creative approach to using numerology to find your soul's mission. Urging readers to 'remodel' their lives and laying out the steps to do so is truly Felicia's gift on her 3 Path life mission. The author has created beautiful living spaces many times in her life and now brings this brilliant metaphor to numerology. This book will inspire and delight you to fulfill your own hidden potential and have fun doing it. Well done, Felicia!"

—SUE FREDERICK, author of *I See Your Dream Job*
& I See Your Soul Mate

"For those interested in knowing themselves better, this is a fascinating, fun exercise. Numbers mysteriously reveal valuable insights. Often, results are dead on."

—FAITH FREED, psychospiritual practitioner and author of *IS: A*
Street Smart Guide to Inspire Your Spiritual Side

"Felicia's insights have inspired me to redesign my life, transforming from real estate developer to the developer of a new food company. Knowing my numbers and the numbers of those close to me has helped me define what I'm doing, and given me the strength and focus to move forward with success. I love the practical way *Redesign Your Life* can help provide clarity and point to deeper meaning behind what I'm doing. It also helps me understand other people in my life in a significant way. I highly recommend this book."

—BOB VONESCHEN, founder and CEO, Bolder Bob's Foods

REDESIGN
YOUR LIFE

Enjoy!

Quinn

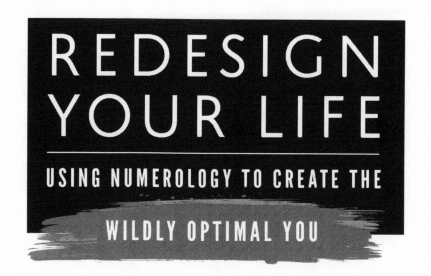

REDESIGN YOUR LIFE

USING NUMEROLOGY TO CREATE THE

WILDLY OPTIMAL YOU

FELICIA BENDER, PH.D.

Boulder, CO
Website: FeliciaBender.com

ISBN 978-0-9851682-0-9

1. Numerology 2. Self-help 3. Life transformation 4. Life coaching
5. Life strategy 6. Emotional healing 7. Relationships

Cover and interior design: *the*BookDesigners
Editor: Stephanie Gunning
Photo of Author: Andrea Flanagan

To Miranda and Phoebe:
You inspire me and make me laugh

CONTENTS

Stop Guessing, Start Living

HAVE YOU EVER asked or heard the question "Wouldn't it be nice if life came with an instruction manual?" The amazing thing is: It does! *You came on a mission.* Even though it's not tattooed on your body, you have a specific purpose in life. You're an amazing person, with phenomenal potential, born with your life's "job description" fully accessible to you through an avenue we'll be discussing in this book: numerology.

In order to live your optimal life, you simply require the right tools to understand who you are and a commitment to work with your inherent strengths, tendencies, and obstacles. The science of numerology offers you those tools, which you may apply to anything you want to change, improve, or create from scratch. It's my mission here to show these tools to you and inspire you to put them to good use. It's my passion to validate your innate gifts and talents, help you set goals for what you want to achieve in life today and tomorrow, and teach you to recognize and overcome your road blocks. In this book, you'll be working through a series of profound, but simple, practical steps as you work on redesigning your life.

Would you like to stop guessing about what you're supposed to be focused on and discover how to feel "on purpose" in your life? Is there something specific in your life that you would like to change? Are you eager to pinpoint your strengths and tame your obstacles? Are you ready to anchor yourself in your true nature and construct some parameters around your choices? If this sounds good to you, welcome to the "Redesign Your Life" center for transformation!

This book is designed to support you in mindfully constructing the wildly optimal *you*. Just like you would if you were redesigning a home, you need a plan to redesign your life. Uncovering your authentic purpose and passions is the first step in developing a blueprint for the person you would love to be and leading the life you would love to live. Numerology is an incredibly accurate resource that can help you devise a solid plan of action. I have used it successfully both in making changes within different areas of my own life and when consulting with clients on small-, medium-, and large-sized life redesign "projects." I like to differentiate the scale of transformations as *redecoration, remodeling,* or *renovation.*

So what is numerology? Numerology was developed around 530 B.C.E. by Pythagoras, a Greek mathematician, philosopher, and mystic. Among many other theories, Pythagoras suggested that each number not only represents a quantity (one apple, two apples, and so on), it also carries a vibration that has a particular meaning and influence on us. Much like gravity or the mystery of cell phone reception, we don't have to understand how it affects us or even to believe in it for it to operate.

This is the short version of Pythagoras' story. If you're interested in learning more about the origins of numerology, refer to the Recommended Resources section at the back of this book.

Like other "ologies," numerology is a vast and intricate art and science. I want to stress the fact that I'm not a professional numerologist, but a life and career coach, so this isn't intended to be a book about numerology in its entirety. In this book I am focusing on only *three aspects* of numerology that you'll find particularly useful as you redesign your life. These are your Life Path Number, your Personal Year Cycles, and your Life Stages and Challenges.

In *Redesign Your Life* you'll learn how to calculate your personal numbers, and you'll be provided with detailed descriptions of what they mean for you. My approach here is a practical, contemporary process using an ancient system as its framework.

Why Redesign?

LOOK AT REDESIGNING your life this way: You've spent years constructing yourself. You have created a job, a marriage, children, or something else. You've selected hobbies, developed likes and dislikes, and placed meaning on each of your past experiences and interactions. You've created your body. You've created the way you relate to yourself and others. Whether or not you're ready to admit it, you've constructed your life and reality up until this point. Sure, you've faced limitations and external influences have definitely contributed to the shape of your life, yet despite (and also because of) those limitations and influences *here you are.*

Where you are now is where you have to begin every redesign project.

If you think of yourself as your house—it's where you live, after all—you can start to work with the idea of redesigning your life. Just like you would if you were to think about remodeling your home, when you ponder the implications of redesigning your life, you have some of the same considerations. First, *you have to want to do it*. Plain and simple.

I'm sure you know people who somehow live in the same house all their lives: the one with the original orange shag carpet, the brass hardware and fixtures, the brown vinyl flooring, and the split foyer. They don't want to change anything! They like their house the way it is and no one can convince them that they might get more enjoyment out of it if they invested in a new coat of paint or a different style of carpeting. They just *don't see* that it's cluttered or outdated. They see their home as a nest of stability, something they can rely upon in an unreliable world. I heard someone say this the other day and it stuck with me: "The more things change, the more *I* stay the same."

Do you know people who fit this description? Are you this person? If so, consider how much additional joy you might get from living your life if you were to take a conscious look around. Perhaps there's something you'll want to do, change, or you might want to add an element to your life to that you can't even imagine quite yet.

Other people know they want to make big, sweeping changes. Usually when people plunk down money for a book about improving their lives, they're ready to make substantial changes. Or at least they're ready to explore their options. Is this true for you? Do you need a little shift or a major overhaul?

It's my purpose in this book to provide you with some engaging ideas, practical examples, and new ways of making the expansive changes you would like to make in your life. If you feel you're living short of the optimal *you*, using your new tool of numerology in tandem with your basic redecoration, remodel, or renovation process will yield you positive, tangible results.

HOW THIS BOOK IS ORGANIZED

Redesign Your Life is structured in three parts that are a logical progression. Part One, "The Preliminaries," lays the groundwork for how to approach change. It covers important questions you must ask any time you prepare to redesign your life and explains that:

- If you need to do a minor change in your life = redecorate.
- If would you prefer a more expansive change = remodel.
- If you're living a life where you don't even recognize yourself anymore and you require a more dramatic transformation = renovate.

In chapter 1, "Setting up Your Project," you'll be asked to define the problem, imagine possible solutions, and—most importantly—figure out whether you are ready to embark on your intended project. To evaluate your readiness, you will be asked to determine your "budget," meaning, *what* and *how much* are you willing to invest as you manifest this change in your life? You will ask yourself to define the scope of your transformation.

The core of the book, Part Two, "Your Numerology Toolbox," outlines and defines three numerological tools. I've chosen these particular tools to give you a major shortcut to the answers you need. Knowing your numbers strips away the endless confusion of competing choices that often leaves people paralyzed. Most people who get stuck do so because they feel overwhelmed. They end up living by default, making few or no choices, or if they do choose, their choices are often made hit or miss without real intention or direction.

The first tool you'll learn, in chapter 2, is your Life Path Number. This is the most important element in establishing your anchor into your true purpose in life. It offers you a framework, foundation, and parameters for your upcoming transformation.

The second tool you'll learn, in chapter 3, your Personal Year Cycles, is a system for working with the flow of your life rather than paddling upstream against the flow. Everyone experiences nine-year cycles that immerse them in different energies during different years. By knowing the numbers related to the years in your cycles, you can enjoy a more effective and satisfying journey.

The third and final numerological tool you'll learn, in chapter 4, is your Life Stages and Challenges. Every life stage has its own challenges. Calculating your Life Stage Number and identifying the challenges inherent within those stages is not so much a predictive tool as one that offers support and guidance for decisions and actions. This tool can be used to map out a detailed vision of your past and future and help you clarify your goals. Knowledge of your Life Stages and Challenges is a platform upon which you can construct your life in a more conscious and meaningful way.

Part Three, "Your Redesign Project," teaches you how to develop a personal blueprint for transformation that's based on the information you've gleaned about yourself in Part One by assessing your desired changes and in Part Two by learning your numbers. Will you redecorate, remodel, or renovate? That's your decision. You'll be most effective if you focus on doing something specific. It's at this point where you'll begin to put your new tools of numerology into play as you develop and then execute a plan for making changes in your life.

Imagine that you've determined you want to redesign your house. What scale of change are you intending to make? Do you want to 1) bulldoze the whole thing—undeniably the most dramatic and expensive choice—and renovate? 2) put in a new kitchen, but leave everything else alone—and remodel? Or 3) get new curtains and make a commitment to buy fresh flowers every week—redecorate? In *Redesign Your Life,* you'll be able to set the scope of your own project. Maybe you want a new job. That could be a renovation project. Maybe you want to set some boundaries around the job you already do in your current workplace. That could be a remodeling project. Maybe you just need a new piece of equipment to make doing your job easier. That's a redecoration project. "The Preliminaries" is where you'll define your project.

Won't it be much more effective if you start your project with a clear goal in mind? By no means does that mean that your plan won't change or evolve along the way, yet things will end up a bit more to your liking if you create a solid vision that focuses on what you truly want.

Is this a Do-It-Yourself Project or will it require some outside help? Will you need an "architect" (a business coach, for instance)? "Contractors" (a personal trainer or therapist, for instance)? How much time, money, and energy will you need to spend on this project? You'll be asked to assess your desires and delve into what kind of commitment it might take to get the results you want. One of the primary issues as you redesign your life is *support.* What does support look like to you? How do you tap into your sense of worthiness and commit to knowing you deserve the change you seek?

If you're interested in redecorating some aspect of your life, you can most likely successfully complete that project solo. Chances are, though, that doing a remodeling or a renovation project by yourself is not possible. Sometimes it takes another person to "hold the ladder," if you know what I mean. So as you redesign an aspect of your life, you'll have to come to terms with the kind of support you'll need and discover how to get it.

Life redesign projects are about process. This is the part no one really likes very much, yet it's the tiger you can learn to tame if you come to grips with the inevitable reality that there'll be glitches

7

and surprises along the way. Your tools of numerology will help you see, acknowledge, and embrace your inherent tendencies and prepare yourself to face the obstacles you'll most likely encounter over and over again on your path to complete your project. In Part Three, "Your Redesign Project," you can step back, define, and refine your personal blueprint, and evaluate where you are in your process: What has been accomplished? What items are left to be done? What kind of maintenance plan do you need to keep moving in the direction you want to go?

Most of us have had the experience of saying we wanted something different in our lives, yet, when it got right down to it, we wanted something to change *without having to change anything about ourselves.* Ever noticed how that just doesn't work? If you want more money, for instance, you may have to do a variety of things in order to get it. Bags of money aren't likely to fall from the sky into your lap. If increasing your income is your redesign project, you'll have to change your *relationship* with money. Maybe that means quitting your current job and hunting for a new one. Maybe it means keeping the job you have while going back to school, and starting your own business. Maybe it means getting a job for the first time. The short of it is: You'll have to place your focus and some energy on earning money in *a way that you haven't before.* Are you ready to alter some of your habits, whether they are mental habits, physical habits, or both?

Part Three is about creating a sustainable "new you." Isn't that what transformation is about ultimately, living as a new person under new conditions? This section offers practical solutions to overcome the obstacles you're bound to face as you follow through on your project, and how you can develop momentum. As you move forward to redecorate, remodel, or renovate your life, it'll be vital to tweak, expand, and update your blueprint.

The goal is to have a blueprint that accommodates the twists and turns that your life brings you.

As you work through the recommendations in this book, you'll discover that redesigning your life is a never-ending process. More than that, you'll discover that you can actually find joy and meaning in redesigning it over and over again, rather than dreading change or looking at planning as a chore. With the proper tools under your belt, your personal blueprint and your new purposeful approach to your life, creating the wildly optimal *you* just got easier.

My Story

WHAT DO I HAVE to offer you as you're searching for an effective way to redesign your life? Frankly, I have been required—like you—to revamp my life periodically. Early on in my life I operated in many ways by default. I grew up with alcoholism, divorce, and other challenging circumstances in my household. My parents divorced when I was ten, and my mother moved me and my two sisters from a suburb in Los Angeles to a very small town in the Midwest. And I mean *small:* population 8,000. To say the least, I experienced a culture shock.

My mother was a single, working mother in the 1970s, overwhelmed by responsibilities and overtaken by addiction. Our family was in a tenuous situation and my mom and I had a strained relationship. My sisters and I were always walking on eggshells. I graduated high school. I got a bachelor's degree in theatre and moved to California to start an acting career. Then I moved back to the Midwest when my former professor asked me to marry him. He was brilliant, old enough to be my father, and I was smitten.

As a girl, I never thought of myself as a woman who would get married early, yet by marrying my professor right after graduating college, I chose to forgo my lifelong dream of becoming a movie actress to be a faculty wife and mother. My husband and I had two beautiful daughters. I didn't pursue a career working outside the home. Nonetheless, I went back to graduate school and got two advanced degrees. Then I worked as a teaching assistant for very little money, mostly assisting my husband.

A major turning point in my life came in the early 1990s. At that time I was both working toward my Ph.D. and being a full-time mom. I was also experiencing turbulence in my marriage, something I wasn't in any way ready to deal with. And by turbulence, I mean *I* was feeling turbulent. While I was dynamic and expressive in academic and public situations, in this intimate relationship I had no core and no ability to express myself authentically.

Less than a year before defending my dissertation, I contracted a rash on my eyes. I went to see my doctor. She gave me a prescription for cortisone, but the cream didn't work. If the rash had been anywhere other than on my face, such as on my back, legs, or abdomen, I would have ignored it. The rash kept on. Applying the cream just made it sting. While I was suffering from this rash, I got a phone call informing me that my mother was in the hospital with a brain tumor, which was the result of undiagnosed lung cancer in an advanced stage. I flew to Arizona to visit her in the hospital, a feat in itself because she was not speaking to me at the time. That visit was strangely surreal.

When I got home, a friend urged me to get a massage to help me relax (I wasn't able to sleep) and recommended a massage therapist to me. This kind of "self-care" was unheard of to me at that time, yet something possessed me to make an appointment. The massage therapist asked me if I'd ever experienced energy work. *Deer in headlights.* "No," I answered. She suggested that perhaps she could do half a session of massage and half of energy balancing. I said okay.

What I remember most about that visit is that there was a poster on the wall in the massage room that read: "How Do You Feel Today?" with about 25 cartoon faces illustrating various facial contortions with an emotion beneath each labeling it: "Frustrated," "Angry," "Sad," and so on. She asked me how I felt. My answer was, "Fine." I didn't notice that "fine" wasn't a choice among the emotions on the poster until she pointed it out. When she did, I recognized that I was in trouble. It was clear I needed help to explore what was happening to me emotionally. From then on it wasn't simply a *want*, it was a *driving need*.

Now, back to the rash. After more time spent learning about energy and healing, I was able to begin to distinguish my emotions on the most basic level. Finally, I was able to realize that my marriage wasn't what I wanted it to be and that I was heading toward either a divorce or another huge change within that relationship. As corny as it may sound, as soon as I admitted what was going on inside of me and could "see" that my marriage was a problem, I woke up the next day and found the rash around my eyes gone. Seriously, it was *gone*.

Though I would not leave the marriage for another nine years, simply allowing myself to recognize the problems in my relationship as a huge issue of concern was what that rash was all about. My rash became an "emotional barometer" for me. It would pop up now and again as a reminder down the road.

My mother died at the age of fifty-nine, the year I battled the unrelenting rash. That same year, a few months after her death, I earned my doctorate. Because of unresolved issues with our relationship, I then started down a path of learning everything I could about the healing arts. I trained and became certified in an energy healing modality called pranic healing®, which I practiced intensively.

Over the next nine years, I ran a spiritual gauntlet. My marriage was becoming ever more untenable. I questioned my life. I struggled to find a job while simultaneously resisting the notion that my marriage was unraveling and my whole life mutating. I was depressed, desperate, and experiencing health problems. I became obsessed with uncovering my passion. Every time I got my annual social security report I would weep. I felt virtually worthless.

Flash forward. After eighteen years, I finally garnered the courage to leave my marriage. That was the most painful, difficult, heart-wrenching thing I've ever done. Before leaving, I had earned a license to sell real estate and started working. Ending the marriage was like jumping off a cliff—a big, adventurous, scary, exhilarating cliff. My daughters were in middle school and high school then, yet their relative maturity didn't make their parents' divorce any easier on them. This was undeniably a huge transitional time for our family.

Through some twists and turns, I ran across information about numerology. It clicked. I had read many spiritual books, so I was no stranger to a vast array of spiritual teachings. Earlier I would never have pulled a numerology book off the shelf; it just didn't speak to me. Probably because—let's face it—I hate math! Numbers had always been my nemesis. In grade school, math was my most anxiety-producing subject. And yet when I opened myself to this information, I found it was intriguing in the same way that the energy healing techniques had been for me. I learned that it's a system that virtually anyone can master *and it is undeniably accurate*. Soon I started coaching individuals and teaching groups on how to use numerology in a practical way to better your life.

In *Redesign Your Life,* I am taking everything I've discovered in redesigning my own life and working with my clients, and offering it to you so you may use it for your benefit. The impact of understanding numerology is that I operate from an authentic and purposeful level on a daily basis. For me, numerology has been a gift that:

- Reminds me of precisely who I am.
- Gives me validation when I am working in the optimal energies of my Life Path Number. How does this validation work? I *feel* content, on purpose, satisfied, and deeply joyful.
- Redirects me when I stray from the constructive use of my skills and talents. How does this redirection work? I *feel* off path, agitated, stressed, and unfocused. When I revisit the defining qualities of my Life Path Number, I can see exactly when I am working with destructive energies and then focus intently on cultivating constructive energies instead.
- Supports my choices by revealing my core purpose in life.
- Encourages me to make mindful choices by anchoring me and giving me parameters in my life within which to function.

My personal and professional lives have been enriched exponentially by using numerology to help me acknowledge and understand the actions I've taken in the past as I work to create an optimal present and future. What I love the most about numerology is that it's simple. *Simple, not easy.*

When I look back at myself even five years ago, it's as though I am now living an entirely different life. My life redesign process has been profound. I have seen it work for myself. I have seen it work for clients. I am passionate about sharing the information with you. I wish I'd known about this shortcut earlier in my life, but I am grateful that I have it now.

How to Stop Guessing and Start Living

THIS ENTIRE BOOK is meant to be a workbook, yet writing on the pages of a book can get messy. You could also be reading the book electronically. Therefore, you can go to my website (FeliciaBender. com) and download a workbook that accompanies *Redesign Your Life*. This is free of charge. Fill out as many worksheets as you need to as you plan and execute your life redesign project. Use them to set up your own personal *Redesign Your Life* notebook.

I have constructed this book to be as practical and user-friendly as possible, including actual case studies as examples and offering exercises and tips along the way. Though you will no doubt be reading this in order to get a handle on your own life, if you're a parent like me you may find that this information is an invaluable tool for understanding and effectively supporting your children on their chosen paths. It can help you understand your friends, family, and co-workers better and foster more effective, authentic, and intimate communication with them.

I'll remind you more than once: What you're working to master and accomplish—as indicated by your Life Path Number—will also be the most difficult or challenging task for you to accomplish. That's why it's called a "lifetime" and not a "weekend workshop." Your life is meant to be your classroom and your playing field. It's where you develop aspects of yourself that usually start out undeveloped. Learning takes a lot of trial and error. It takes time. It takes resilience.

Wouldn't it be bizarre to expect a newborn baby to drive a car? Nonetheless we often expect ourselves to attempt similarly miraculous endeavors. We are unhappy with some aspect of our lives and yet we demand that we jump from point A to point Z in one swoop. That's rather like asking a new baby to grab the keys and drive to the store to pick up some milk. We must be aware that a lifetime is a long growth process with rich and delicious opportunities along the way that require us to develop skills and maturity over time.

As you apply the numerological information about your Life Path, Personal Year Cycles, and Life Stages and Challenges to your redesign project, you'll gain the freedom that comes from refining and honing in on an exact pool of choices. I find it tremendously reassuring to know that there is truly a time and a "season" for everything. Knowing your cycles as defined by your numerology has the potential to give you permission to take the time you need to create a rich tapestry of life experiences. My goal is for you to take guessing out of the equation and begin your life's redecorating, remodeling, or renovation project with direction and gusto. As you embrace your redesign process you'll start living more profoundly and mindfully. Just remember to take time to enjoy yourself along the way because redesigning your life starts right now.

PART ONE

THE
PRELIMINARIES

CHAPTER 1
SETTING UP YOUR PROJECT

SO WHY DID YOU pick up this book? What is it about the idea of redesigning your life that piques your interest? Are you trying to decide what to declare as your major in college and have no clue what that might be? Perhaps you'd like to change your career and haven't yet found a way to do it. Are you on the brink of a divorce and looking for ways to avoid it or to make a smooth transition out of your marriage? Do you feel stuck and frustrated because you don't really know what you want in your life? Are you simply curious about numerology and want to find out more about it? How about the idea of improving and adding to the things that are already working for you?

If any of these statements describes where you are emotionally or practically at this moment, then the Preliminaries is the perfect place to start reading. Every time you have a new change to make in your life, a new redesign project, always begin at the beginning again.

To help you align with what you would like to focus on in your life, please take the time to complete the following Redesign Startup Survey. Use this as a gauge to assess where you are emotionally, physically, spiritually, and financially. Before you start putting tools into your redesign toolbox, you need to strap on your apron or tool belt and get ready for your project. Taking the time to answer these questions will help get you into the groove to move forward. Fill out the survey and then hold on to your responses. You'll "score" your answers and use them to guide your forthcoming project.

Redesign Your Life Survey

Circle the number below each question that best describes you right now. One signifies that this statement is entirely inaccurate. Ten signifies that this statement is entirely accurate.

1. I FEEL "STUCK."

1   2   3   4   5   6   7   8   9   10

Never an issue   Sometimes an issue   Consistently an issue

2. I GET SIDETRACKED WHEN I ATTEMPT TO CHANGE MY LIFE FOR THE BETTER.

1   2   3   4   5   6   7   8   9   10

Never an issue   Sometimes an issue   Consistently an issue

3. I HAVE A HARD TIME LETTING GO OF THE PAST.

1   2   3   4   5   6   7   8   9   10

Never an issue   Sometimes an issue   Consistently an issue

4. I FEEL OVERWHELMED.

1   2   3   4   5   6   7   8   9   10

Never an issue   Sometimes an issue   Consistently an issue

5. I'M DISSATISFIED WITH MY LEVEL OF FINANCIAL INCOME.

1   2   3   4   5   6   7   8   9   10

Never an issue   Sometimes an issue   Consistently an issue

6. I FEEL THAT I'M NOT DOING WHAT I'M MEANT TO BE DOING IN THE WORLD.

1   2   3   4   5   6   7   8   9   10

Never an issue   Sometimes an issue   Consistently an issue

7. I WISH I'D MADE DIFFERENT CHOICES IN MY LIFE.

1   2   3   4   5   6   7   8   9   10

Never an issue   Sometimes an issue   Consistently an issue

8. MY EMOTIONAL CONNECTION WITH MY INTIMATE PARTNER NEEDS IMPROVEMENT.

1   2   3   4   5   6   7   8   9   10

Never an issue   Sometimes an issue   Consistently an issue

9. I WOULD LIKE TO IMPROVE MY RELATIONSHIP WITH MY PARENTS AND SIBLINGS.

1   2   3   4   5   6   7   8   9   10

Never an issue   Sometimes an issue   Consistently an issue

10. I'D LIKE TO UNDERSTAND MY CHILD(REN) BETTER.

1   2   3   4   5   6   7   8   9   10

Never an issue   Sometimes an issue   Consistently an issue

11. I'D LIKE TO COMMUNICATE WITH MY FRIENDS MORE EFFECTIVELY.

1   2   3   4   5   6   7   8   9   10

Never an issue   Sometimes an issue   Consistently an issue

12. I WANT TO EXPRESS MYSELF IN A MORE AUTHENTIC WAY.

1   2   3   4   5   6   7   8   9   10

Never an issue   Sometimes an issue   Consistently an issue

13. I MAKE DECISIONS BASED ON FEAR.

1   2   3   4   5   6   7   8   9   10

Never an issue   Sometimes an issue   Consistently an issue

14. I HAVE A LOT OF REGRETS.

1   2   3   4   5   6   7   8   9   10

Never an issue   Sometimes an issue   Consistently an issue

15. I OFTEN FEEL FRUSTRATED.

1   2   3   4   5   6   7   8   9   10

Never an issue   Sometimes an issue   Consistently an issue

Now add together all the numbers you circled. Write your total below.

YOUR TOTAL SCORE: _____

THE MEANING OF YOUR RESULTS

HERE'S WHAT YOUR score means: redecorate, remodel, or renovate.

If you scored between 15 and 45: Consider a redecoration project. Chances are you feel on target in your life most of the time. Yet sometimes issues come up, things to evaluate and change, shifts that you want to make as you go along. So if you answered the bulk of the questions in the "never an issue" range, you'll be able to calculate a gentle, minimally invasive, and easily manageable shift in some aspect of your life.

If you scored between 46 and 105: You're distinctly in the "it's time to remodel" camp. Remodeling your life will require a bit more staying power than a redecoration. You can expect some peaks and valleys as you traverse this transformation; some a bit easier, some a bit harder to pull off. I'd guess that the majority of people who feel compelled to pick up this book are in this stage. Some serious shifts need to take place in your life.

If you scored between 106 and 150: You're at the apex of a renovation period in your life. This is a time in which everything is up for grabs and you're feeling bad, uncomfortable, or numb. You now have an amazing opportunity for self-reinvention. If you're experiencing a major health problem, tremendous emotional pain, a spiritual crisis, a financial emergency, or you're in the midst of an intense relationship transition, you're in the perfect place for an "all or nothing" or "it's now or never" transformation.

While change sometimes feels excruciating while it's happening, the result can be nothing less than miraculous when you move through it and come out transformed on the other side.

Defining the Scope of Your Redesign Project

AS YOU BEGIN your personal redecoration, remodeling, or renovation, it's imperative that you consider the scope of your project. This means sitting down and, as clearly as possible, mapping out the parameters of your project. Based on the metaphor of home construction we're using, this means delineating the different line items in your plan. For instance, how much money, energy, and time are you willing to "pay" for the plans (reading this book, taking a class, and acquiring other information you need to transform your life), what is your scope of work (redecorate, remodel, or renovate), and what's your ultimate vision for your final product (how do you envision your life changing?).

You'll need to establish a timeline of specific milestones you must hit to complete your project, and to assess who needs to be on your support team (for instance, a doctor, a web designer, or an office assistant).

Basically, the needs of this process also demand that you achieve clarity about your overall purpose for redesigning your life. What do you really want? How can you begin to shift your perspective about issues that have held you hostage for years? How can you begin to think differently about them so that you can truly change your life?

Interestingly, I have found that often it's difficult to focus on the actual "thing" that can help us move forward in making changes with the most success. Many clients who come to me for coaching have layers of issues in their lives that make it challenging even to know where to start. For instance, the main goal might be *to find a way to work at home and make a six-figure income.* And yet, as we unwrap the layers surrounding this desire, we discover complex issues. Let's say you're a single mom living with your parents, who are helping you raise three children, two of whom have special needs. Your husband left the marriage after you found out he was sexually abusing one of the children. You're still dealing with the court system with this issue. You have a low-paying job you hate and are trying to take some classes so you can retool your job. Oh, and you're fifty pounds overweight. Where would you begin?

If this scenario sounds exaggerated to you, be thankful. There are many people who find themselves in similarly intense circumstances. If this scenario sounds too close for comfort to you, then take heart.

You aren't alone. Invariably, the best place to begin is *within you rather than outside of you*. So given this particular scenario, rather than making your primary goal a big leap into making a six-figure income as an at-home entrepreneur, I'd suggest that your success would rise exponentially if you started with a more manageable goal. Perhaps you'd begin by focusing on gaining control of your health and committing to a weight loss program. Just that alone could create a chain reaction in your life that would move you forward in ways you can't imagine, even though initially it sounds much less exciting.

After you have success at taking control over your health, you would experience a great boost of self-confidence and a feeling of being more energetic and powerful. Losing that first twenty-five pounds could very well offer you the fuel to continue moving toward some of your other goals more easily. *The key to change is to break down your goals into manageable, doable steps or action items.*

A great way to feel less overwhelmed about getting started is to segment your life into four basic quadrants: career/finances, relationships, health, and spirituality. It might look like this:

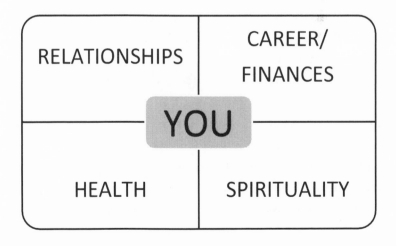

Breaking your life into quadrants is a simple way to come to terms with the layers that are involved with what you would like to change in your life. When you can work with segments rather than with *everything at once*, you're much more likely to have success. Otherwise, you're likely to end up feeling paralyzed and unable to move forward. So in other words, your plan for how you choose to redesign your life won't be determined by a "one size fits all" approach.

Another major point I want to make is this: While it helps to pare down your focus by choosing career/finances, health, spirituality, or relationships, you may find that your project will consist of an intersection of more than one of these quadrants. Yet it always helps to start by focusing on just one.

For instance, say you're waking up with migraine headaches everyday and you would like to do something about that. If you're using that issue as something you'd like to redesign, then you'd place that in the "health" quadrant. And yet as you start filling out your "Redesign Your Life" homework, you see that you started having migraines when you got a new boss at work who you don't like. You also see that for the past year you've dreaded going to work more and more every day because you're getting frustrated with your job and wish you could quit. So while your migraines certainly are a health concern, as you dig deeper, you'll discover that the migraines are the result of your discontent with your job: In order to get rid of the migraines, you might have to get rid of your job. At the very least, you'll have to change something about your job to relieve your discontent.

I also feel that ultimately everything boils down to one thing: relationships. Everything about your redesign project has to do with your relationships with money, with your health, with food, with intimacy, with your sense of worthiness, with your family, with yourself. So even though we'll attempt to lasso something specific as your starting point, expect your issue to overlap and be prepared for some surprises along the way.

Before we delve into the tools of numerology, let's break down your project into a small, medium, or large undertaking. Having a good handle on the scope of what you want to accomplish will be key in achieving the change you want to make, and then sustain, in your life.

Project: Redecorate

WHAT I LOVE about redesigning a life is that a project can be about adding one more wonderful improvement to the life you already feel passionate about. You don't have to be desperate or require monumental change to make good use of your numerological toolbox. In fact, when you're someone who already feels "on purpose" in your life—meaning, when you feel good about most aspects of your behavior and want to take more powerful steps forward in the direction you're already going—numerology adds depth to your understanding of yourself and others. It's a shortcut to making the great parts of your life even more enjoyable because it helps you to identify and work with your inherent tendencies. Knowledge of the parts of you that might benefit from a tweak here and there gives your efforts a little *oomph.*

So if you are in this arena, congratulations! I bet it's safe to say that you've made a conscious commitment to yourself and have spent a good portion of time doing a lot of work spiritually, emotionally, physically, and even financially to achieve this. So guess what? Whatever you've been doing is working. As you move forward with your project, I'll ask you to add the tools of numerology to your toolbox so you can enjoy even more profound and rapid growth.

Perhaps you know that one quadrant of your life is lacking more than the other three. In this case, you can easily locate your most problematic issue and focus on it. If you're already clear about where you are and what you want, you're certainly a step ahead of the crowd.

Working on smaller changes or transitions in your life is a project for "redecoration." In terms of construction, this would mean that you're already living in your house or apartment; it's pretty well updated and in proper working order, and both the exterior and the interior are clean and pleasant. The only thing you feel a burning desire to do is to paint the living room a richer color. Or perhaps your home office needs to be cleaned and rearranged. Maybe it's time to replace the old blinds with curtains. In any event, whatever you're working on is a smaller change or addition, something that isn't drastic or absolutely necessary. Rather, you want to redecorate to improve the space, making it feel more beautiful and comfortable to you, and basically letting it become a more pleasing place to live that'll more accurately reflect who you are.

In terms of your life, if we apply this same idea, it means you're just making tweaks. You could be in a phase of life, for instance, in which you'd like to explore your spirituality. Maybe you feel solid and directed in your career, you're happy with your relationships, and your health isn't a problem, yet you're yearning to expand yourself in an intangible way. Suddenly you find you're meeting people who are engaged in healing practices that are new and interesting. Or someone loaned you a book on intuition, quantum thought, or numerology and you feel intrigued and ready to learn more. That's a redecoration project.

Let's say you're feeling called to shake up your workout routine. A new yoga studio has opened around the corner and you're thinking about taking classes there even though you've never taken a yoga class in your life. That's a redecoration project.

Maybe you're going through some personal stress—not major, but noticeable—and decide to try meditation for the first time or want to commit more fully to practicing meditation more than you do already. This would certainly be a redecorating project for you, since expanding on something you already do is additive. Change doesn't necessarily have to be driven by angst or a lot of pain.

While spiritual growth or a change in your fitness program may remain a redecoration project for you, there is also a chance that the growth you experience may lead you into a remodeling project later on.

If you are in a redecoration phase of your life, chances are you feel:

- Your life is generally on track.
- You know what your purpose and passion is and you are acting on it every day.
- Generally healthy.
- Grounded and supported in your spiritual life.
- Most of your relationships are positive.
- Excited about finding new activities to pursue.

Project: Remodel

IF YOU FIND YOU REQUIRE a medium-sized shift in your life, I call that project a "remodel." Most of us go through several remodeling projects in our life spans—how many you've already been through depends on your age. The truth is that most of us reinvent ourselves over and over again, whether we engage in these transitions mindfully or go kicking and screaming. It's not news to anyone that change is the only constant in life. Even so, working through our inevitable changes can be tricky, especially when the circumstances that initiate them are painful.

When you remodel your house, it's obviously a bigger undertaking than redecorating it. It requires concentrated thought. Remodelers must have drawings and plans to communicate their desired changes to everyone who'll be involved in the construction. A remodeling project requires thought about a budget. When you redecorate, you may have a lump sum earmarked for your curtains, then you buy and install them, and—*voila!* —you're done. By contrast, remodeling involves more intricate planning, changes, rearranging, and higher expense.

A good example is what happens when you're remodeling a kitchen. Will you change out the old appliances, put in new countertops, resurface the cabinets, and add a new backsplash? In addition, do you want to tear out the floor and put in new tile, rearrange the counters and install an island, and replace the old cabinets with brand-new ones? Certain degrees of remodeling require more thought, energy, effort, commitment, patience, money, and follow-through than others. A bigger remodeling project always requires involvement by other people, whether they are family members helping you out or subcontractors you hire.

Do you know what else is inherent to a remodeling project in a house? Problems cropping up, frustrations, delays, course corrections, and communication issues—and the original budget is often exceeded. Whether you are talking about a home redesign or a life redesign, as your project becomes larger, so do the complications associated with getting the job done and getting it done right. That's where breaking down the project into smaller portions is the key to enjoying a satisfying result rather than ending up with a sloppy mess.

As a real estate agent, I showed a lot of fix-and-flip properties to potential buyers. Over and over, we'd walk through homes where the owners had started to remodel, run out of money, and given up. Sometimes they didn't hire professionals and got in over their heads, doing such a horrible job that it was sadly laughable: We'd see grout between tile two inches wide, beveled molding that didn't match or come together in the corners, or my favorite, *carpet that was caulked together.* Yes, caulked! You can see a photo of the actual caulked carpet to which I'm referring in the Redesign Your Life workbook. Go to FeliciaBender.com to download your copy.

In terms of your life, a remodeling project results in a medium-sized change, such as quitting a job and getting another, returning to school to get a certificate or a degree, having a minor health issue that requires some changes in your diet and exercise program, or any other situation that demands a fairly substantial shift in the way you live on a daily basis. When you remodel your life, you're going for a lasting change, not for a little addition or tweak to what you're already doing.

For example: Meredith found that when she turned forty-six, everything changed for her. She didn't believe in all that "hormone and aging stuff" she'd read about until she woke up one day and found out that for the first time in her life she needed reading glasses. Not only that, she was getting softer around the middle. Meredith described the appearance of her abdomen as "cottage cheese." Rather than just drift along with similar impending changes, Meredith renewed her resolve about taking care of herself. Having been pretty good about her diet, exercise, and personal self-care, Meredith decided to be proactive and remodel her exercise regimen. She realized that what had worked for her before just wasn't cutting it with her shifting hormones.

Meredith set up her action items in alignment with the changes she wanted to make in her physical body and in her mental health.

Frankly, she was a bit miffed about having to age. She worked at remodeling her routine. She started with beefing up her exercise routine to five days a week rather than three. She devoted herself to doing some challenging workouts that allowed for cross training: These included cardio, weight lifting, and yoga. She reserved space at her house for her workouts. She remodeled her diet, focusing on eating small portions at frequent intervals during the day. She also read books and articles about menopause and perimenopause so that she could feel more knowledgeable about what she was experiencing.

While it may sound like it was pretty easy, Meredith remodeled her daily routine in a dramatic way by adding more exercise and committing to a long-term change in the way she operates her day-to-day life. This wasn't a project that was a one-time deal and then back to business as usual. Meredith changed her life, stuck with it, and incorporated the changes into her daily routine. That's the hallmark of a remodeling project.

The point is this: Remodeling your life requires a bit more know-how than redecoration. It just does. A lot of people jump into remodeling with great enthusiasm and then don't have the commitment to stick with the project and solve problems that crop up along the way. That's why you have to prepare yourself by getting clear about what you want. Otherwise you won't be able to communicate your vision to others, and you won't anticipate how much effort and tenacity it will take from you to work through the project to completion.

If you are in a remodeling phase of your life, chances are you feel:

- Your life is slightly off track.
- Confused about your purpose and passion—different enthusiasms come and go.
- You have some health issues.

- Unsure about your spiritual beliefs or are working on expanding them.
- Some of your relationships need work or evaluation.
- Slightly overwhelmed, yet focused on finding new and exciting ways to improve your life.

Project: Renovation

NOW FOR THE PROVERBIAL Big Kahuna. If you find yourself at a crossroads in life where things *must change* and they *must change in a big way,* you're in a renovation stage. You may want and need to make massive changes and other personal renovations at various points in your life. As you begin to learn about numerology, I'll introduce you to two specific times in your life when you can expect to feel an urge to renovate. These are called "Saturn Returns." The end of a nine-year Personal Year Cycle always brings major changes, too.

I consider renovation projects life transformations that are all-encompassing and life-altering. For instance, major health issues, major accidents, a death in the family, a job loss or career change, a spiritual crisis, or a bankruptcy. These are the sorts of heightened and urgent issues or transitions that change a life forever. I can't leave out the more intense reasons for renovation, like going to or coming out of prison, going to or coming home from war, dealing with any bizarre crime perpetuated on you or a loved one, recovering from a suicide attempt, or any other dramatic and traumatic event. All of these types of experiences demand a monumental renovation.

If you're thinking: "Oh my God, I'd rather die than renovate my life! It sounds horrible!" then hold on a second. I know it sounds like something to be avoided at all costs, yet it's not. When you're facing renovation, you can be sure that if you forge through it with conviction, on the other side your life has the potential to be incredible. It'll look like something you could never have envisioned when you were living in your old comfort zone.

A major theme in numerology and in this book is this: *Growth doesn't take place when you're sitting in your comfort zone.* You experience the most profound levels of growth when you're smack dab in the middle of pain and discomfort. That's when change happens. That's when core learning takes place. That's when you see what you're really made of. Anthony in the 2011 film *Lost Christmas* says it eloquently: "Sometimes you have to go toward the things that make you want to run away." When you're renovating your life, this is imperative.

In the 2011 movie *The Beginners*, Christopher Plummer plays a man in his seventies who comes out of the closet as a gay man after his wife dies. Talk about a renovation! What a profound shift in his life and, by extension, in the life of his adult son.

Consider how Pema Chodron, an American woman who had two children and two divorces, became a Buddhist nun at midlife. You can't tell me that was a logical or easy choice for her to make. Yet she found her calling and became an influential teacher, writer, and speaker who engages audiences with Buddhist thought and teachings. Becoming a nun was a drastic departure from the life she'd been living. From an outside perspective, it might have looked like an easy shift. Yet the renovation she and her family experienced was life altering for all of them. There was the picture of before, which looked one way, and the picture of after, looking entirely new.

There are lots of examples of people dramatically altering their lives due to extraordinary circumstances. While it may sound sensational, think about the well-known child actors who suddenly find themselves unemployable as adults and have to reinvent themselves. How about professional athletes whose sports careers have ended? Or wealthy people who suffer financial loss and have to come to terms with their lives in a way they have never had to before? Lottery winners who become overnight millionaires? The dramatic changes these people have to make would qualify as life renovations. Something similar may have happened to you or someone you know. Major transitions happen in people's lives all the time.

Numerology can help you find outlets for your great skills and talents, and support you in the demanding process of renovating your life. Undergoing a dramatic life transition often is a catalyst for people to recognize their power and purpose suddenly with a lightning bolt of clarity. I have met people who passionately devote themselves to the mission of charitable organizations because they had a traumatic personal experience that the organization helped them manage. From that moment on, they had a driving passion to speak, act, and contribute. John Walsh, host of *America's Most Wanted,* would never have become involved in a television show if he hadn't endured the kidnapping and murder of his son.

Think of Christopher Reeve, Michael J. Fox, Elizabeth Glaser, and countless others, both living and deceased, who have devoted themselves to ground-breaking medical research due to their private battles with serious health conditions. The point is this: While it's never the easy route, renovation is a profound eye-opener, wisdom-bringer, teacher of life lessons, and intense mental clarifier.

If you are in a renovation phase of your life, chances are you feel:

- Your life is turning upside down.
- Frantic or cynical about your purpose and passion.
- You have major health issues.

- Severely tested about your spiritual beliefs.
- Almost all of your relationships are mutating.
- In "fight or flight" mode or knowing that it's "now or never" to make huge changes.

Other Considerations: Budget, Timeline, Support

AS YOU DETERMINE the scope of your project, there are a few more considerations. You've set boundaries around the size of your project: redecoration, remodel, or renovation. Now you need to work at setting your budget, deciding on a timeline and milestones, and clearly defining how much and what type of support you need in order to get the job done. Resolving such matters is imperative as you hash out your plan for achieving what you'd love to see as your end result.

Setting your budget: The first element in any redesign plan to consider is its expense. If the scope of your project is a "redecoration," your budget will be relatively low. How much will it cost? How much money do you need to be prepared to spend to get what you want?

Your expense could be the cost of a book, the cost of a coach or counselor, or the cost of tuition for a class. Whatever you tangibly need in order to redecorate your life, budget for it. If weight loss is your project, there are different ways to reach the same goal. Will you join a gym, and if so, how much does a gym membership cost? Do you need to buy workout clothes? If you intend to exercise at home how much are you budgeting for DVDs, music, and equipment?

Deciding on a timeline and milestones: Next you need to plan your time and energy. Are you budgeting to clear your calendar for a whole weekend in order to get a redecorating project done from beginning, middle, to end? Will you need to take more than one weekend, or even to schedule a few days off work? The amount of time you require is the next item in your budget.

It's always best to be realistic about your timeline. If you don't give yourself enough time, you're doomed to failure or a half-baked result. Additionally, you'll have a tendency to engage in your project with a sense of hurried urgency. That sort of pressure rarely elicits the most creative mindset. Alternately, if you give yourself all the time in the world without a deadline, chances are your efforts will stall or fade away.

You must set up a timeframe in order to gain momentum with your project. Goals and action items within a timeframe can provide you with the structure you need to move forward rather than hover or tread water. Consider the milestones you need to hit and when each will be done.

Labor is a matter of energy as well as time. If your completion date is near, the energy you expend may have to increase. If you completion date is far off, you may expend less effort.

What kind of a shift are you making? Are you going to give yourself only a week to lose ten pounds? Not likely. So how long will it take? Can you commit to clearing an hour every day or three times a week to devote to this enterprise?

Defining how much and what type of support you need: Following money and time, make a plan to get the support you need. Are you going it alone or will you ask your friends and family to support you? Will you ask your sister to help you make the color choices? Maybe you want your kids and husband involved and, if so, in what manner? You'll need to plan job descriptions and make sure you're all in agreement (or at least on the same page) about what's going on.

In terms of support, the key question is: *What does the support you need look and feel like?* Several years ago, I was dating a wonderful man. I remember talking with him about something challenging I was going through and he asked: "How can I support you with this? What does my support look like to you? Have you ever allowed support into your life?" I don't know about you, but that was the first time anyone had ever asked me those simple questions. I wasn't prepared to answer at that point. So I went and thought about it and got clear on what support looked like for me. But not only that, I asked myself, "What would support *feel* like?"

Many of us are used to feeling as though we have to carry the load by ourselves. That's why we feel so darn tired all the time. I guarantee that you'll experience deeper success when you're able to ask for what you want and then accept it graciously when it's given to you. Allowing good things into your life may sound easy, yet I'll guarantee that single act alone requires a huge leap in the way you think about yourself. Allowing support means you know you're worthy and deserving of the transformed life you're envisioning and creating.

Feeling our own sense of worthiness is something we all grapple with in our lives. The sense of unworthiness we dip into on occasion manifests itself in various ways, ranging from self-sabotage to cynicism and victimization. Allowing support into your life is a more substantial issue than it might appear on the surface.

The flipside of this scenario is being a person who expects other people to do it all for you. Instead of relying on yourself most of the time, you expect others to support you, help you, and smooth the path for you. If this has been true for you, that in itself is a clear reason to redesign your life. Either you feel somewhat empty and powerless, and would like to feel purposeful and powerful, or the people in your life who've enabled you have stopped doing so and you feel lost and angry. Either way, the result is the same. It's time to sink or swim. Chances are, if you're seeking help, you'll soon be mastering the skills to swim. Hang in there!

It's time to figure out what support looks and feels like to you in the most optimal and empowering form, so you can ask for it, be receptive, and embrace it when it starts infiltrating your life, especially when that means asking it of yourself before you expect it from others.

Then there's another question to keep in mind. What if I don't get the support I'm looking for? How will that lack of support effect my projected goal? This is important. I fully believe that most often we find the support we're looking for when we ask for it and allow it in. And yet, there are times when you just aren't going to hear "rah-rahs" you might be looking for from those around you, especially family members. Remember, as you change, those around you must change in response to you. It's as though you're the nucleus in a cell and, when you mutate, so must all of the other organelles around you (in this case, friends, colleagues, family, and supporters). While *you* may be ready for a big change, the people around you might not be quite as excited about it because it means they have to reevaluate aspects of their own lives that they might not be eager to face.

Because your resolve will undeniably be tested—an important factor to identify when you think about what support looks and feels like to you. You'll be challenged to become strong, resilient, and committed to fostering positive change in your life. You'll be offered many opportunities to work around other people's opinions of the changes you're making. Every fear you have about making this change in your life will be offered up to you on a platter. You'll hear every "rational" reason why this won't work, why you should stay put, why you shouldn't rock the boat, why you can't dare change the dynamics of your relationships. Ultimately, when you ask yourself what support looks and feels like, your primary goal is to envision yourself supporting *you*, being solid, steadfast, empathetic, kind, and tenacious. That's the *you* that you want on your support team. After you come to terms with what support for your project looks and feels like to you, then it's time to deal with your mental devils: pesky fear-filled thoughts that infiltrate our minds, grab on to our expansive ideas, and mangle them into oblivion. You know exactly what I'm talking about. Playwright Eugene O'Neill called these negative and paralyzing thoughts "formless fears." Now you'll be asked to examine the formless fears that are holding you back from moving forward on your redecoration, remodeling, or renovation project.

There's always a fear of some kind that aims to keep us stuck when we *really* want something else. We call them reasons, excuses, practicalities, "I can'ts," or any other rational or irrational explanation as to why we should just stay right here, right where we are.

"Don't move! Don't even breathe!" is what that formless fear is telling you in your head. Now is the time to dissect your fear and acknowledge what it is, where it lives, what it thrives on, and where it came from. Only then can you neutralize the tremendous power it wields over you.

The final phase as you outline your project is to consider your first action items that will start your project moving forward. Remember when we talked about taking "smaller bites" at the beginning of this chapter? This is a simple way to bring your project into action by focusing on manageable steps you need to take as you begin this journey of redecorating, remodeling or renovating your life. How many action items you start with really depends on you, the size of your project, and whether you're easily overwhelmed or thrive on direction and homework.

Some people resist homework and some love it. If you resist the homework idea, write down one to three action items to begin. If you love homework, start with three to five action items. Either way, write them down. *Give yourself a goal and a deadline to meet that goal.*

40

Then your task is to be accountable to yourself to get it done.

This is when knowing yourself and your tendencies comes in handy. If you're a person who has trouble maintaining direction and focus, you'll want to take a leap and ask a friend or hire a coach to help you stay on task. Perhaps you'll thrive by setting up a Redesign Your Life meet-up group with like-minded friends in order to support each other through your process. If you thrive by setting goals and marking them off your calendar, then you can most likely do this with great success by simply taking the time to write it down and take yourself and your redesign project seriously.

The idea is to break your project down into manageable segments. When you complete the first several action items, cross them off your list (crossing the completed tasks off a list with a bold colored pen always feels so great), and then write down your next several action items, remembering to clearly define your goal and the deadline. This will be how you work through your project from beginning, middle, to the end. We'll go into more detail about how to manage this in later chapters, after you learn more about your tools of numerology.

You Deserve Everything Life Has to Offer

I KNOW THAT BREAKING DOWN your project in this way may seem arduous. Yet working out a projection of your goals and steps, and visualizing your results is the ticket for achieving your intended changes. This will help you develop a process that clicks for you and leads you toward the results you want. As you practice defining your scope of work for whatever you want to redesign right now, and then do the same thing over and over again in the future, it'll become an easy ritual. These are simple steps—simple, not easy. It takes commitment, practice, and the right tools to take your life to the next level.

41

Many of us don't feel we deserve to be happy or successful. Even if we say we do, internally we often don't really believe it. Our negative beliefs about our worthiness are what keep us in the familiar place of "not good enough."

When you dig into your numerological toolkit, it's my fondest wish that you use the information to really, truly, madly, deeply embrace the fact that you are spectacular. Not just all right . . . *spectacular*. Yes, you have issues. Yes, you've done some stupid things in the past. Yes, you want to be a better person. Nonetheless you were born to add your unique and wonderful gifts to the world. Everyone is. You can validate yourself with numerology, a great way to start knowing—down to your core—that you're worthy of every fabulous thing life has to offer.

Ultimately, we experience all three types of redesign many times throughout our lifetimes. It's great to learn powerful tools that help us navigate our transitions with ease and mindfulness. There are times when that small redecoration project is exactly what we need to shift into an even more positive track. Remodeling happens whenever we go through major cycles of change in our lives.

Statistically, 45–50 percent of first marriages end in divorce. Almost half of us, therefore, experience a divorce, an event that definitely requires a remodel or a renovation. But wait, there's more. According to Jennifer Barker at the Forest Institute of Professional Psychology (www.divorcerate.com), 60 to 70 percent of second marriages and 70–73 percent of third marriages end in divorce. I was rather shocked to learn this statistic. Obviously most of us don't get better at marriage with more practice. Divorce alone constitutes a major turning point in life that many people experience either in a remodeling or a renovation stage.

Now having worked through the preliminaries, it's time to open your toolbox and get a handle on your numerological tools.

The next three chapters are designed as a reference guide for you. Initially, you may focus only on understanding your own Life Path Number, Personal Year Cycles, and Life Stages and Challenges. In fact, that is what I fully expect you to do: to find *your* numbers and soak in your own personal information. See how the information resonates as you use it to develop a blueprint to redecorate, remodel, or renovate your life.

PART TWO

YOUR

REDESIGN TOOLBOX

CHAPTER 2
YOUR LIFE PATH NUMBER

MOST PEOPLE EXPERIENCING a desire to redesign their lives are feeling off track somehow in subtle and not-so-subtle ways. If this is true for you, rest assured that once you become familiar with your Life Path Number you'll know where to place your attention in order for this to change. You can experience amazing shifts. Most people experience a *zing,* a sense of validation they've been seeking, or an immediate sense of clear direction and getting back on track by learning their Life Path Number.

Your Life Path Number provides you with a trajectory for your life and information about what you're here to experience. There are nine basic Life Path Numbers (counted 1 to 9). Your Life Path Number is a key to understanding your life purpose, innate tendencies, talents, and the obstacles you'll face in creating your optimal lifestyle. Not only does your Life Path Number suggest what you were born to accomplish, it's helpful in predicting stumbling blocks. Bear in mind that what you've come to do will be a challenge. It always is.

In addition, many people have a Master Path Number.

Some numerologists work routinely with Master Path Numbers. For the purposes of this book, I'll outline the defining qualities of Master Numbers 11/2, 22/4, and 33/6. I won't go into as much depth about the Master Numbers as I will the numbers 1 through 9, because the Master Numbers take their primary essence from the defining qualities of the single-digit numbers 2, 4, and 6. Then I'll explain the additional qualities a Master Number brings to the mix.

As career intuitive Sue Frederick would observe: Don't have path envy! Having a Master Path Number isn't better or worse than having a "regular" number. In fact, if yours is a Master Path Number, it means you have intensified obstacles as well as heightened potential in your life. One number is never *better* than any other. Each has a unique vibration that carries a particular meaning. We're here to learn the things that our own vibration brings.

I'll explain how to calculate your Life Path Number presently.

In redesigning your life, your goal should be to establish and maintain a balance between the *constructive* and *destructive* aspects of your number. You could also call these aspects "positive/negative" and "underactive/overactive." Your Life Path Number paints a wonderful picture of what's possible when you embrace and understand your core mission. When you operate out of resistance and fear, as we all do at certain points during the course of a lifetime, chances are you're working with the destructive tendencies of your number rather than operating in the expansive energies the constructive aspects bring to the party.

You might take a look at the description of your Life Path Number and question it because you don't feel it describes you accurately. In fact, you could feel that you're the opposite of what your Life Path Number says about you. Let's say, for instance, that yours is a 3 Life Path Number. A 3 Life Path is all about communication and emotional self-expression. But you're scared to death to speak in front of people and feel rather detached emotionally. Not very 3-like.

So you'll perhaps say that the number can't be right. In this case, you're experiencing what I'd call the flipside energy of your Life Path energy. This indicates to me that you're probably engaging with the destructive aspects of your Life Path Number much more consistently than with the constructive aspects. The way I can know for sure? I'll ask you if you're happy and satisfied with your life. My impression will be validated if the answer is, "No" or at least, "Not so much."

Because people often experience both the constructive and destructive aspects of their Life Paths, in this book I'll focus both on what you look and feel like when you're working with the most constructive elements of your number, and then I'll also focus on what you look and feel like when the default mechanisms of the destructive aspects come up.

What I most often hear from people who learn their Life Path Numbers for the first time is: "Oh, my gosh! That's so crazy! No wonder I'm [fill in the blank]." There's often a sense of relief because the number validates what they already feel inside. As they learn more about the tendencies and obstacles of their Life Path, they become more aware of their challenges and hone in on how to bolster their innate skills and talents. I expect your process to be similar.

There are times when you'll feel as though you're jumping through rings of fire when you work with your numerology to redecorate, remodel, or renovate some aspect of your life. Yet the redesign process will feel exhilarating as the rewards start rolling in. If you're a 5 Life Path (which is all about fearlessness, freedom, and adventure) and yet you hyperventilate at the thought of packing your suitcase, you'll feel so much more authentic and alive when you can work through that issue rather than avoiding it or making excuses for it.

The key here is that you'll finally be able to realize that your debilitating fears around this particular issue are a key to your redesign process, not just a random fear or random "throw-away" issue. What I mean to stress here is that when you discover you're a 5 Life Path and that the primary mission for you is to develop your sense of freedom through self-discipline, some of your consistent issues can very well start making a lot of sense to you in a way that has potentially eluded you before.

So look at it this way. It's like *Goldilocks and the Three Bears*. You're Goldilocks. Your Life Path is like all those choices you have to make in the story between the three bowls of porridge, the three chairs, and the three beds. When you choose the one that's too hot, too big, or too hard, you're operating in the destructive, or overactive, aspects of your Life Path vibration. When you choose the one that's too cold, too small, or too soft, you're operating in the destructive, or underactive, aspects of your Life Path vibration. When you choose the one that's *just right*, then you're operating in the balanced or optimal aspects of your Life Path vibration.

While it's a constant challenge and negotiation to remain balanced in life, you'll be guided toward making the balanced decisions by *keying in to how you feel*. When you feel off, you're making choices that are off. When you feel good, empowered, and on target, you're making *just right* choices more often than not. How you feel is the most reliable measure of your state.

The information conveyed here may or may not resonate with you at this particular time in your life. Some traits that are outlined may not be dominant for you or perhaps show up in different ways. I find that certain elements speak to people at different times in their lives, particularly given their age. If you're in the early stages of your life, you'll experience the information differently than you will in the middle or later stages of your life. This will become even more apparent in the chapters on the Personal Year Cycle and the Life Stages and Challenges.

At the end of each section describing each Life Path Number I'm adding a small section that is specific to each path that offers insight into your particular road to redecorating, remodeling, or renovating your life. I figure, if everything were hunky-dory you wouldn't be spending the time and energy to read this book, so I'm offering a glimpse of some of the ruts in the road and Life Path-specific issues you might find yourself experiencing and wanting to address.

The key to using numerology to create the wildly optimal you is this: When you understand the key elements that make up the constructive elements of your Life Path and then are able to apply that knowledge to your everyday life decisions, and even more importantly to your everyday *way of thinking*, numerology can clear away the debris that stands in the way of you getting what you really want out of your life.

How to Calculate Your Life Path Number

TO CALCULATE YOUR Life Path Number, simply add the numbers of your birth date together. Your goal is to finish with a single-digit number. So if there is a double-digit number at the end of your first calculation, it's an intermediate number. Do one more step of calculation that leads you to a single-digit number.

EXAMPLE: BIRTH DATE JUNE 18, 1990

6/18/1990

$6 + 1 + 8 + 1 + 9 + 9 + 0 = 34$

$3 + 4 = 7$

Number 7 Life Path

For the final number to be accurate, you must use all of the digits from the year of your birth. You can't use 6/18/90, for instance, since that's missing 19 (for the century) and skews the results.

If your Life Path Number is a 2, 4, or 6, you will need to do two additional calculations to determine if your Life Path Number contains one of the Master Path Numbers: 11, 22, or 33. These are double-digit numbers that show up in the first round of your addition process.

EXAMPLE: BIRTH DATE DECEMBER 3, 1960

12/3/1960

$1 + 2 + 3 + 1 + 9 + 6 + 0 = 22$

22 is a Master Path Number

$2 + 2 = 4$

Master Life Path Number 22/4

If you have a Master Path Number, also calculate by the number of the month (in this case 12), by the number of the day (in this case 3), and by the number of the year (in this case 1960) to see if the Master Path Number 11, 22, or 33 shows up again.

$12 = 1 + 2 = 3$ (the month is a 3)

$3 = 3$ (the day is a 3)

$1960 = \quad 1 + 9 + 6 + 0 = 16$

$1 + 6 = 7$ (the year is a 7)

Then add your final numbers together (month, day, year) to get your ultimate result.

$$3 + 3 + 7 = 13$$
$$1 + 3 = 4$$

Calculated this way, you can see there is no Master Path Number elsewhere in your number.

You can also calculate your Life Path Number as follows:

$$
\begin{array}{r}
12 \\
3 \\
+\ 1960 \\
\hline
\end{array}
$$
$$1975 = 1 + 9 + 7 + 5 = 22$$
Master Path Number

$$2 + 2 = 4$$
Master Life Path Number 22/4

The Life Path Reference Guide that follows describes the defining qualities of the 1–9 Life Path Numbers, as well as of the Master Path Numbers 11/2, 22/4, and 33/6. Pause and calculate your Life Path Number. Then turn to the section of the reference guide that pertains to you.

With your Life Path, there are optimal ways to work with the vibration of the number. You have challenges and tendencies that are specific to your path. What should be stressed here is this: Whatever path you're on will seem to be *the most difficult thing for you to do.* That's why it's called your "Life Path," because it is a lifelong journey and won't be accomplished during a weekend workshop. Issues in your life that present themselves as challenges will come up over and over again until you develop a certain acknowledgement, understanding, and mastery of them.

LIFE PATH REFERENCE GUIDE

1 LIFE PATH: The Leader

Personal Mission: To Develop Creativity and Confidence in Every Aspect of Your Life

A born leader, you're self-motivated, independent, and a hard worker. You thrive in a competitive environment, although you often get sidetracked by listening to the non-stop voice of criticism in your head, whispering incessantly: "You're not good enough." Make sure to practice turning the channel when you start listening to that station. That voice isn't telling you the truth. It's a decoy that leads you away from your true power.

As an individualist, you've most likely felt unique in many ways. When you're feeling insecure, you feel you just don't fit in or belong anywhere, as though you're really out of sync with the demands and expectations of the world. When you're being your authentic self, you're the kindest, most trustworthy, compassionate, and compelling individual. When you aren't feeling confident, you tend to be pushy, defensive, aggressive, and angry. Those emotions are your chosen outlets when you're having self-doubts.

It's crucial for you to work on honing your skill at anything you do, whether that means your job skills, communication skills, or relationship skills. Reaching a level of expertise instills you with a reliable sense of self-confidence. As a 1 Life Path, having complete trust in the skills you've learned and mastered will serve as a kind of "security blanket" for you when you're feeling insecure or your sense of confidence is under fire. Having the ability to fall back on high-level skills you know inside out will stabilize you and get you back in your game.

You're a pioneer, an innovator, and capable of great success and achievement in the world. You need to be in charge and managing in some way. You would make a great entrepreneur or inventor. Often the highest and best use of your abilities is when you mastermind a project, get it up and running, make sure management systems are in place, and then you're off to the next venture. You might feel stagnant if you don't allow yourself to tackle new challenges.

You're full of creative energy, so embrace your creativity and understand that this is your gift. Imagine new things, introduce new concepts, and then delegate the details and either move on with another project or continue developing your project while taking it to the next level of success. However you define it, you enjoy being on the move and having a variety of things to do.

Anything that calls for tapping into your unique voice, independent action, and decision-making is your forte. When choosing a career, you must ask: "What is it I've always wanted to be or do?" and then *just do it*, like the Nike slogan commands. Really, nothing can stand in your way. Whether or not you know it, you have an amazing capacity to do whatever you focus on after you clear away the clutter of self-doubt. When you're secure in your abilities and have confidence, you're fabulously dynamic.

You also—whether or not you know it yet—have healing hands. You're a natural healer and can use this ability in every aspect of your life. You don't have to become a massage therapist or an energy worker unless you want to. That's not what I'm saying. Healing energy surrounds all aspects of what you do and guides your actions when you're functioning optimally.

As you develop your leadership skills, nurture the best in others and understand that creativity flourishes in an atmosphere of inner security and confidence; meaning you must open up, take risks, and step off the beaten path. Your constant challenge is to consistently and consciously develop your sense of being self-assured, self-directed, and centered. When you express your passion from the heart, you can achieve great things in the world. Be careful of succumbing to feelings of superiority, judgment, and criticism. You're most effective when you work directly with people and key into their innate gifts and strengths.

The late Steve Jobs (born February 24, 1955) was traveling the 1 Life Path. He exemplified the energy of the rugged individualist who followed his own unique voice no matter what other people thought. Like Steve Jobs, if you have a 1 Life Path, you have lots of ideas and need ways to express your amazing creative voice. And, most likely, other people will clamor to copy your success after you work out all the kinks.

George Clooney (born May 6, 1961) also has a 1 Life Path. Perhaps you're similar to him: magnetic, devoted to causes you feel passionate about, and willing to forge a path and become a leader to achieve the results you envision in your mind.

Common threads when a 1 Life Path is "on fire" from working with optimal energies are boldness, innovation, risk taking, resilience, and following the inner voice.

Your life purpose is to bring positive creative energy into the world.

1 LIFE PATH: Potential Challenges
Your potential challenges are:
- To come to terms with insecurity and the tendencies to block, withhold, or discharge energy through addictive behaviors.
- To acknowledge that when you lack self-confidence you're lured into inaction and stagnation.

- To realize that if you're not using your creativity you're prone to feel lethargic, frustrated, or held back.
- To understand that you may appear to have a chip on your shoulder, as if you have something to prove to yourself and to others.
- To understand that when you feel under fire, you default into negativity, judgment, cynicism, and anger and aggressively express those feelings to others.
- To know that you excel in creative problem-solving, yet often lack the confidence to express and capitalize on your innate skills.
- To know you tend to experience crippling self-doubt when dealing with something new.
- To appreciate that action and ambition are key components of who you are and aren't to be avoided.
- To work constructively with the fact that you don't like to be told what to do.
- To make sure to choose partners who are your equals both in intimate and in business relationships. You won't have satisfying partnerships if you choose to partner with people who are weaker or more submissive than you.
- To comprehend that when you're working with destructive tendencies you lean toward self-absorption, self-interest, cynicism, and selfish focus.

1 LIFE PATH: Strengths to Develop

- The "confident you" has unique perceptions, style, and magnetism that attracts others. Always trust and follow through on your unique visions. You aren't meant to follow the crowd.
- You're dynamic when you're working with confidence. Remember you're a trailblazer. Since you're on the front lines,

you'll experience a lot of "failures" and stumbling blocks. So what? Those experiences can fuel you to develop new ideas and follow through on your revolutionary projects.

- You're resilient. You're knocked down over and over again in your life. Know that you're going to get more than your share of this. You're not going to think it's fair. The key is to learn from your failures rather than be devastated by them.

- You're a whiz at accomplishing a multitude of tasks. When you set your mind to accomplishing something and go about it with direction, confidence, and empathy toward others, you're working optimally.

- You're a creative problem-solver. Give yourself lots of pats on the back for a job well done and for bouncing back from adversity. Work on letting yourself hear positive affirmations in your head rather than self-deprecating and self-defeating "tapes."

- Creativity in all forms is at the core of your being. Enjoy and embrace every opportunity to use your creativity.

1 LIFE PATH: You Know You Need to Redesign Your Life If . . .
If you can identify with the core issues presented in these examples, knowing the key attributes of your 1 Life Path will help you identify your patterns and offer you some satisfying alternatives.

PROJECT: CAREER RENOVATION
You're working at a job that doesn't tap into your creativity or your leadership abilities. If you're a 1 Life Path working as a secretary, behind the counter, or in other jobs that are more detail or service oriented and less creative and synergetic, you'll most likely have a desire to redesign this part of your life.

PROJECT: RELATIONSHIP REMODEL

You're in relationships where you don't feel confident in yourself, so you've developed a "victim" mentality. Meaning, you might use your intelligence to find every negative aspect to government, to your work environment, or to the way your family behaves. Rather than seeing the more positive aspects in life, you operate with a sense of superiority, sarcasm, cynicism, and a sense of defeat.

PROJECT: RELATIONSHIP RENOVATION

You're operating full-throttle and with high levels of success in your career, yet your personal relationships are either non-existent or unhealthy. You can't seem to stay married for long or just don't get far enough into intimacy to get married, staying in the "just passing through" zone in your relationships. While people admire you and what you accomplish in your work and career, you might be known as someone who is difficult to get along with and not much of a team player.

2 LIFE PATH: The Mediator
Personal Mission: To Develop Cooperation and Balance in Every Aspect of Your Life

You're a seeker of harmony and deeply loathe conflict. While you usually do whatever you can to avoid conflicts and confrontations, sometimes you take the opposite route and are very combative. When you're combative and agitated, you can be sure you're responding to situations in a reactionary way rather than in an empathetic or give-and-take manner.

You're happiest when you're being of service to yourself, your family, your group, or when you're excelling in a service-oriented career. Working in a group environment is often the best for you to achieve success. You're the detail person, the one everyone turns to in order to get the job done and get it done right. You thrive in an environment of support and solid direction, so you may not enjoy working for yourself or might not find ultimate success or happiness as an independent contractor.

The energy of the 2 life Path is *very sensitive*, so much so that you get your feelings hurt every day in ways no one but you can understand. Even you don't understand the degree to which you're emotionally wounded day in and day out. Truly, your heart is on your sleeve. You're super aware of what's going on in everyone else's emotional life and often take it on yourself.

Your tasks are: 1) to realize that you're hypersensitive and that other people don't necessarily see the world and take it in the same way you do, and 2) to construct your own set of "psychic armor" to protect yourself from the onslaught of emotional energy you take in daily. Only with protection can you find healthy balance.

The 2 energy is all about *love*. You're here to love others and be loved in return. Do you know the song "I Want You to Want Me"? That defines you. You crave giving and receiving unconditional love. That desire combined with a strong sense of service and emotional sensitivity brings amazing things into your life, as well as consistent challenges. The trick is not to focus on needing love to the point of desperation.

Since you're so sensitive and also want to give and get love all the time, you may have a tendency to smother your loved ones or have expectations that can never be met. On the flipside, you may back away from wanting love because it hurts too badly. When you can come to an understanding about how to balance your intense need for love, you'll feel secure and supported. The trick for you is to give yourself the acknowledgement you need, rather than seeking it from outside sources.

You contain a powerful combination of strength and sensitivity that doesn't always show on the surface. The 2 Life Path tends to gravitate toward family life. You often serve as a supportive, dependable, caring helpmate when you're working with your most positive aspects. You don't necessarily enjoy the spotlight and have a tendency to get angry if you feel pushed or threatened.

Your trademark is a tendency to do everything for everybody to the point where you feel drained. Even though you're here to serve and love, from the outside people may observe that you give yourself a little too much credit. You aren't meant to receive intense validation from external sources. Why not? Because learning to give yourself your own kudos is part of the challenge of the 2 Life Path.

Oftentimes you judge yourself on what everyone else says or thinks about you. Your challenge is to develop your internal compass and turn inward for validation. You must be careful not to take on the problems of the people you love, who are more than happy for you to do so. It's best not to place yourself completely at the disposal of others because soon you'll get angry and resentful for being used and unappreciated.

When you're clearly on task, you're luminous, content, and satisfied with life. Knowing that you're here to serve, love, and be of use to yourself and to others will keep you focused on the constructive aspects of your Life Path.

When you end up living in the destructive aspects of the 2 energy, no one knows what you want, including you. You're too preoccupied doing what you think you're supposed to do and are quick to expect others should do the same. You're in a chronic state of codependence. Your giving turns to resentment, as you give too much, and then you withdraw completely. Only when you realize you're totally free to form your own life through your own sense of internal guidance, while detaching from your skewed sense of what others expect from you, can you truly reach your potential.

It's interesting to look at well-known people and investigate the 2 Life Paths, because there are less 2s in the "famous" arena than some of the other more flamboyant Life Path vibrations, simply because 2s don't really seek the spotlight.

Yet perhaps you can relate to Julie Andrews (born October 1, 1935), a talented and demure 2 Life Path whose most famous roles were a reflection of the cooperative and harmonious energies of her Life Path Number. Think of Maria in *The Sound of Music*, Mary Poppins in *Mary Poppins*, or Victoria in *Victor/Victoria*. Andrews' presence is calming and unifying in her screen roles. Or perhaps you can see yourself in Sidney Poitier (born February 20, 1924), another 2 Life Path whose screen presence reflected a calm, yet intense persona.

Common threads when a 2 Life Path is working with optimal energies are groundedness, fair-mindedness, service orientation, loving, and being lovable.

Your life purpose is to clarify the limits of your responsibility and learn to work in cooperation with harmony, balance, and mutual respect.

2 LIFE PATH: Potential Challenges

Your potential challenges are:

- To balance your compelling sense of responsibility to others with your own inner needs and limits: finding the balance between giving and receiving, saying yes and no, the value of thoughts and value of feelings, your own needs and the needs of others.
- To let go of the need for approval from others.
- To create an internal sense of integration. It's as though you have two people inside of you, each trying to drive your life. Your task is to integrate these opposing forces into one complete whole.

- To resign from your self-appointed job as "General Administrator of the Universe." Once you do, you'll find inner balance and health, and set an example for others by empowering them to take their share of responsibility (as long as you're able to follow through with love and compassionate detachment rather than with resentment and ego).

- To refrain from over-cooperation, co-dependent relationships, and taking responsibility for everyone else's happiness despite the fact that you don't know what that might really require for anyone else than yourself.

- To stop the internal "should" dialogue. "Should" is a big word of significance for 2s. What others *should* do and what you *should* do.

- To blaze through confusion about what is the "right" decision or action.

- To trust your own inner voice and inner experience rather than looking outside of yourself for guidance and asking everyone else: "What do you think I should do?"

- To get past stubbornness, unfairness, and self-centeredness.

- To modulate your default response: "It's their fault!" While this may elicit others to see you as judgmental, what you're really saying is: "It's not my fault."

- Cooperation will quickly turn to conflict if you begin to feel overwhelmed; then you'll shift into under-cooperation, resistance, or even total withdrawal. You eventually shut down entirely as a way of not only showing your resentment but also as a form of self-preservation. Notice when you're turning this corner so you can rebound faster.

- Know that behind your stubbornness is a feeling of helplessness and a real fear of being over-powered and taken advantage of by others. Yet often you're treated in a way that you have set up yourself, invited, and even demanded. Establish loving boundaries and you'll find you no longer serve as an emotional doormat for others.

2 LIFE PATH: Strengths to Develop

- You feel most satisfied when you're of service in some capacity. You have the drive to serve and help, to instruct and guide, to assist and support.

- You're big-hearted at your core and thrive in taking a step-by-step approach to problem solving. Beware of getting caught up in emotional drama and focus on your goals.

- You're full of compassionate emotions. When you learn to act on the basis of what you truly feel—when you can get down to it—your decisions and your service will last longer. Learning to express your emotions with integrity and authenticity allows you an intense amount of personal freedom.

- You're meant to help people and are at your best when you're using your gifts to help others. You must learn the difference between support and servitude. Only give when you feel energized by giving. Limit your giving when you feel drained.

- While you're innately responsible and reliable, you face a constant push-pull between over-giving and resentment for not being enough, doing enough, being acknowledged as you feel you should be, or being appreciated. Let go of your *exaggerated* sense of responsibility in order to work in your optimal realm.

2 LIFE PATH: You Know You Need to Redesign Your Life If . . .

If you can identify with the core issues presented in these examples, knowing the key attributes of your 2 Life Path will help you identify your patterns and offer you some satisfying alternatives.

PROJECT: CAREER AND RELATIONSHIP RENOVATION
You're a stay-at-home mom and your youngest child just graduated from college. Suddenly you see that you need to reposition yourself and focus on getting a job outside the home, and yet you don't have the slightest idea where to begin. So you end up putting your own transformation on hold. Instead, you keep a tight rein on your kids, spouse, and other family members. Your kids wish you'd stop calling them twice a day and your spouse is playing an awful lot of golf lately.

PROJECT: CAREER REMODEL
You're working at a job that requires independent sales and you keep finding a reason to quit or somehow you get fired, yet since you have experience with this particular job (say as a real estate agent or small business owner), you keep gravitating toward it. But you feel unhappy, unfocused, and unable to close the deals.

PROJECT: RELATIONSHIP REDECORATION
OR REMODEL
You're experiencing a lot of stress because your extended family is impossible to deal with. You plan all the get-togethers, you get all the supplies, prepare it all, clean it all up, write the "thank you" notes, and yet no one understands how much work you put in to make all the family functions operate smoothly. You're sick of it. But you're already halfway through shopping for your parents' anniversary party supplies and are peeved because only one sibling has even sent a RSVP.

3 LIFE PATH: The Communicator

Personal Mission: To Develop Expression and Sensitivity in Every Aspect of Your Life

The 3 Life Path enjoys performing and taking center stage, however you personally define this. You love creativity, communication, and connecting with people. The 3 energy is truly the energy of *joie de vivre* (the joy of life). If you're working the constructive aspects of the 3 energy, you're connected with your emotions—and you have a lot of them. You communicate brilliantly and clearly. You consolidate information easily and know how to rework that information into new ideas. You embrace your brimming creative impulses with gusto.

You're a natural writer, actor, counselor, or professor. Any profession where you can present your ideas to an audience is right up your alley. You aren't a nine-to-five job person; you don't necessarily work well under the supervision of others or within a rigid structure.

Your mind moves so quickly that when someone is slow thinking you easily get frustrated. In communication, you're usually direct and compassionate, yet if you're still developing these skills, your tendency might be to become domineering and to state your thoughts and feelings bluntly, which is hard on those around you. You may end up regretting things you say, so contemplating what you want to communicate and how you want to say it—hopefully in a supportive way, with a little cushion underneath it—will be in your best interest.

This isn't to say you shouldn't communicate your feelings. Just the opposite. Many 3s spend years learning to gauge that they even *have* emotions, and then they spend more years learning how to express them.

One of your biggest obstacles is your intense self-doubt. Feelings of insecurity can stop you in your tracks and literally stun you into submission. While everyone experiences self-doubt at certain times in their lives, this is a ruling factor of your life when you're on the 3 Life Path.

Avoid getting stuck over-analyzing or over thinking every single thing. You'll mud wrestle with "analysis paralysis" over and over again. When you resort to that, you'll drive yourself—and everyone else—crazy. When you experience these feelings, your best action is to *take action*, even when you feel paralyzed. Just moving through the doubt by taking *one step beyond it* will turn what used to be your biggest enemy into your personal house pet.

In relationships, you can be romantic and fiercely loyal. You have a tendency not to let go of past relationships. You mull them around in your head again and again, picking apart things said and done, what could've been and what wasn't. You level blame on yourself and on others.

You tend to obsess over the smallest emotional hooks that bog you in a pool of cynicism or emotional defeat. When you find yourself grinding over an issue and shredding it into a pile of goo on the floor (so to speak), your best solution is just to leave it alone. Just stop. If it's really vital and needing your input, it'll come back into play for you when it's less emotionally charged.

You're a natural counselor who sees potential in others, so you might choose a partner who is a "patient" that you think you can save or fix, either consciously or unconsciously. When you can't, this will lead to depression, which is your malaise of choice. Number 3 Life Paths make the best manic-depressives, experiencing extreme highs and lows. If you're not using your talents, you'll experience mood swings. When you realize that your journey is an emotional one, you can learn how to manage the ups and downs more effectively.

You must be careful about with whom you spend your time because you will attract "takers" if you aren't careful. You must learn to walk away from relationships unbalanced in this specific way.

Overall, you can be the life of the party: clever, witty, the clown, entertaining, and good company. You make a great host or hostess and people feel nurtured and comfortable around you. You make it all look so easy.

In fact, one of the pressures of the 3 Life Path is that you're so good at everything you do you have a difficult time choosing what to focus on. Sometimes you have difficulties following through on plans. You may observe that you just can't decide how to direct your energy and become scattered and ultimately depressed and ineffective at completing whatever you set out to do. So many ideas, so little time.

One of the reasons is that you can talk yourself out of virtually anything. You can find the tiniest fault with your "Big Idea" that stops you from proceeding past the fun part. You like fun and immediacy. Although you have a great amount of reserve and tenacity, you often spend it on other people and not on yourself.

It's not surprising to find many 3 Life Paths in entertainment, politics, or any other industry that requires expert communication skills, intellect, and a good sense of humor. Bill Cosby (born July 12, 1937) is a great example of the integration of the 3 Life Path elements of great sense of humor and quick wit, entertaining and intelligent, making you feel at home in his presence and using his talents to inspire and uplift others. Cosby even earned a doctorate in education where he wrote a dissertation titled, "An Integration of the Visual Media via 'Fat Albert and the Cosby Kids' into the Elementary School Curriculum as a Teaching Aid and Vehicle to Achieve Increased Learning." He has developed the key aspects of the 3 Life Path, using his charisma, intellect, and caring to inspire positive social change.

Actress Cameron Diaz (born August 30, 1972) embodies many of the traits of her 3 Life Path, including her vivacious, freewheeling and breezy personality and her simple joy of living.

Other well-known 3 Life Paths include Daniel Radcliffe (born July 23, 1989), Kate Middleton (born January 9, 1982), and Hillary Rodham Clinton (born October 26, 1947).

Common threads when a 3 Life Path is working with optimal energies are being dynamic, self-assured, joyful, emotionally balanced, expressive, and inspiring.

Your life purpose is to use your emotional sensitivity and self-expression to uplift and heal others.

3 LIFE PATH: Potential Challenges

Your potential challenges are:

- To confront issues of blocked or distorted expression, as well as emotional oversensitivity and self-doubt.
- To grapple with your tendency to see the negative side of things and dwell in negative forms of expression, such as whining, complaining, badmouthing, and criticizing.
- To know that when overwhelmed or feeling stifled, you may withdraw and "clam up," which only serves to punish others for your inability to work through your own feelings.
- To acknowledge that you're an emotional sponge to others' feelings when they're upset or being negative.
- To get past being a perennial student, eternally preparing, picking up advanced degrees and changing course, but never venturing into the marketplace or focusing on something specific, never fully committing yourself.
- To come to terms with the ways in which you are hypersensitive to criticism and often take even the smallest affronts personally.
- To work toward knowing that you tend to misrepresent your feelings and your needs to others and to yourself, which results in communication based on manipulation, hinting,

withholding, or conniving instead of honest self-expression.

- To fully understand that you need to assert yourself and learn to express anger or aggressive energy constructively or else you'll remain inhibited or frustrated in manifesting the full range of your powers.

- To realize that a common scenario for a 3 Life Path who has been emotionally wounded early in life is not to allow yourself to step into your path and embrace your creative self-expression. If you were emotionally wounded as a child, you probably don't feel worthy of embracing your emotions and acting on your creative impulses. If this is the case, you're prone to serious depression and illness because you haven't moved through your fear.

3 LIFE PATH: Strengths to Develop

- Embrace the fact that you're here expressly to be a portal of emotional self-expression. You're at your best when you locate and share your authentic feelings honestly and directly while encouraging others to do the same.

- You're a fountain of emotional sensitivity, therefore you're great at tuning into other people's emotional state quickly and accurately. Most people aren't as acute as you are at reading people's wants and needs, so you're often disappointed that others aren't as adept at intuiting what you need from them. This means you need to clearly express how you feel and what you need, even if you think the other person should know it already.

- Because you're a quick study and master skills easily, you have a tendency to underplay your many strengths. Understand that things you can accomplish easily (and you think everyone else finds easy too) aren't easy for everyone. Since many things come easily to you, it's best if you learn to pare down your focus and commit to going through the steps to fully manifest one thing at a time.

- You're a highly-energized person full of knowledge, creativity, and ideas galore. The only thing standing in your way is you, when you succumb to the forces of self-doubt. To avoid emotional paralysis, keep in mind that taking one small step toward your goal will peel away the doubt and allow you to move forward.

- You're smart. You have a highly charged brain and that leads you to over think virtually everything. Cut yourself some slack, have some fun, enjoy all aspects of your journey. All the bad stuff in your life prepares you by giving you a reservoir of knowledge and experience to help others on their own life journeys. Yours is the path of joy and happiness when you allow it.

3 LIFE PATH: You Know You Need to Redesign Your Life If...
If you can identify with the core issues presented in these examples, knowing the key attributes of your 3 Life Path will help you identify your patterns and offer you some satisfying alternatives.

PROJECT: CAREER AND HEALTH REMODEL OR RENOVATION
You don't understand why you just can't stand being an accountant anymore. You find that you're waking up with migraines, have consistent intestinal distress, and can't see to shake those ten extra pounds you gained last year.

PROJECT: RELATIONSHIP RENOVATION
You've finally admitted to yourself that your marriage just isn't working for you anymore, but you feel guilty because you've tried to please everyone for so long and you haven't expressed your real

feelings to your spouse or to anyone else close to you. You're feeling like a split personality because you're at the point where you just can't take it anymore and yet you don't feel you have the ability to speak up for yourself.

PROJECT: RELATIONSHIP AND SPIRITUALITY RENOVATION

It's been a long time since you thought about what you really enjoy. Things never go right for you and your glass is always half empty. No one understands you and all you have had to endure in your life. Your adult kids rarely contact you because you didn't build a very supportive relationship with them, but you're really angry with them because they obviously don't respect you. The last time you read a book or tried something new was years ago.

4 LIFE PATH: The Teacher
Personal Mission: To Develop Stability and Process in Every Aspect of Your Life

A 4 Life Path is all about developing stability through process. Yours isn't a rambunctious journey; rather, you're cerebral, intelligent, and a seeker of knowledge. If you were to audition for the cast of *Winnie the Pooh*, you would land the role of Owl. Because you know how to build solid foundations, you're often placed in charge of developing operating systems and are expected to look after the details. You're the workhorse and "master builder" of the world.

You devour information so that when you find a topic or subject that interests you, there's no end to the depth of your knowledge about it and your ability to impart that knowledge to others. You're a born teacher. You may not become a teacher in the traditional sense, yet you demonstrate an undeniable depth of knowledge and just can't help sharing what you know with others.

While you can certainly have a sense of humor and moments of lightheartedness, you tip the scales toward seriousness, brainy activity, and rational thought. You may come off as cynical when you offer advice, yet what you're really trying to do is offer information you think will help a person or a situation.

You're the first to say you don't want to argue and yet you most often end up in arguments because you tend to be opinionated about things you feel you know a lot about. You need a lot of positive affirmation and are uncomfortable with, or even afraid of, criticism. If you can't do something perfectly according to your standards, you often don't do it at all. As a result, a lot of your dreams haven't been achieved.

Home is important to you. You crave a sense of security that "home" exemplifies. One of the primary issues faced by the 4 Life Path is the necessity to work through problems with family of origin. While all of us have family history to deal with, the 4 Life Path rides a particularly rough road with family that's at the core of the healing and learning you've come here to do. Many 4 Life Paths have family histories that include literal or figurative abandonment, abusive parents, drug or alcohol abuse by one or both parents, an early death of a parent, and other forms of trauma. In order to work optimally with the gifts of the 4 vibration, you need to look at your wounded or problematic relationships and work through the feelings of lack and pain they've brought to you.

Because of your volatile past, you have a desire to protect— yourself, things, and the people around you. You like things that are tangible and solid. Honesty is crucial to you, especially in relationships. You take in everything and experience a lot of sensory overload. Even though that's the way you process information, it can lead to feelings of being overwhelmed.

Because of the high-intensity way you absorb and process

information, you need to take plenty of time for yourself and cultivate peace and quiet in your environment. This is imperative for your mental and physical health. You have a sensible, traditional, well-behaved way about you and aren't "into" people who are otherwise. You don't understand people who are big risk takers, don't follow the rules, or don't thrive in a traditional work or family environment. You also have a "loner" quality to you. You have no issues with spending time alone.

If you're a woman, you may be strong to the point of being perceived as more "masculine" because of your energy; you take care of everything and are super responsible. Many 4 Life Path women are drawn to intimate relationships with men whom they end up financially supporting.

Sometimes you might lean on alcohol or other calming drugs as a way to relax your constantly moving brain. Yet remember that nature's beauty has a calming effect on you, so use that as your outlet for relaxation.

You feel most comfortable when you're moving slowly and deliberately. You work out your plan and want your life to be orderly. Underneath that planning is a fear of chaos and a real dislike of appearing stupid or naïve in any situation. Overall, you're eminently practical, hardworking, and determined. No matter what, you'll get it done.

I've found an amazing array of well-known 4 Life Paths and I must admit that I'm often surprised to find who is traveling a Life Path with this vibration, from Chelsea Handler (born February 25, 1975) to Bill Gates (born October 28, 1955), Sean "P-Diddy" Combs (born November 4, 1969), and Brad Pitt (born December 18, 1963). Despite their obvious differences, these folks share a life of hard work, a talent for digesting knowledge, a talent for teaching others what they know, and a commitment to (or avoidance of) reaching their goals through a steady and stable process.

Common threads when a 4 Life Path is "on fire" and working with optimal energies are being practical and detail oriented, sharing knowledge, and working to establish a sense of security.

Your life purpose is to achieve stability and security by patiently following a gradual process toward your goals.

4 LIFE PATH: Potential Challenges

Your potential challenges are:

- To embrace the idea that a stable foundation is the key from which all else flows for you. Foundation energy reflects issues with family—either the family you came from or the one you produced.

- To comprehend that because you're here to work toward stability through step-by-step processes, many things test your sense of stability. You may have deep issues with parents and other family members who served as your foundation early in life. You've probably asked yourself more than once: "How the heck did I end up with *these* parents?" Therefore, working out family issues and rebuilding your sense of security forms an integral part of your life's work.

- To confront issues in the areas of stability, commitment, patience, clarity, and willingness to follow a slow process to reach your goals. You need to create a sense of inner stability —physically, emotionally, mentally—before moving forward. "Proper preparation prevents poor performance" is a good mantra for you.

- To beware that the flipside of your hard-working energy is the avoidance of hard work. Do you have difficulty putting down roots and staying put for a while? Do you cringe at the thought of hard work and concerted effort? Then it's your task to understand the value of commitment to things in your life: to a relationship, a present location, to a line of work. You might be surprised at the relief you feel by allowing yourself to commit to something.

- To realize that if you lack physical flexibility, you most often have psychological rigidity as well, manifesting as stubbornness in the form of self-deception or "tunnel vision." You prefer to operate with blinders on, not really listening to, or heeding others' feedback or advice. This often leads to feelings of regret because of opportunities not taken.

- To know that you might have a heavy dose of impatience. Your tendency is to drive hard to reach your goals and then if you don't achieve success as quickly as you'd like to you feel discouraged and say, "What's the use?' or "Just forget it." You may approach relationships in the same manner, starting with intensity and enthusiasm and then abandoning the relationship when problems surface.

- You need a *plan* and the patience to follow through with it because you have tendencies to skip steps on the one hand or get obsessed or stuck on a single step and lose momentum. If a step is skipped, you'll always have to go back and make up for the lost step before being able to move forward.

- You have a surprising amount of stamina, vigor, and fortitude, yet these qualities can sometimes manifest as stubbornness and resistance, making it difficult for you to let go of the past. Often you tend to nurse regrets and have tendencies to obsess on old relationships, mistakes, and failures rather than seeing them as lessons to be used for bettering your life.

- You have a tendency to make the same mistakes over and over again. You may marry the same type of man or woman several times. You may quit smoking and start smoking again and quit again, over and over throughout your life. You might hop from job to job without finding the type of job that you feel passionate about that fits your needs. You may avoid committed relationships again and again until you realize too late that you let real love slip out of your grasp.

4 LIFE PATH: Strengths to Develop

- You make an excellent parent if you've done some good emotional work surrounding your own wounded childhood. Developing your own family is a great way to become the parent you always wished you'd had yourself and give your own children the benefit of your hardship. You can also take the opportunity to parent yourself along the way to make up for what might have been lost during your own upbringing.

- A 4 Life Path needs to focus on practical ways to manifest goals, because you're the one with the plan. Achievements results from clear intent and focused effort *over time*. Your ability to build strong and resilient "things" extends from relationships to business systems to the actual products people use.

- You thrive on responsibility once you get a taste of it, because often it provides you with a sense of stability you so crave. You're the one that people look to for answers and are the solid presence other people count on. Yet often you then take on so much responsibility that you get overwhelmed. Because you need guidelines and limits, and to know what is expected of you, for you the best kind of support can take the form of clear expectations.

- You take comfort in having and living by a clearly defined system of rules. If you don't know the rules, you tend to feel confused.

4 LIFE PATH: You Know You Need to Redesign Your Life If . . .
If you can identify with the core issues presented in these examples, knowing the key attributes of your 4 Life Path will help you identify your patterns and offer you some satisfying alternatives.

PROJECT: CAREER AND RELATIONSHIP REMODEL OR RENOVATION
You're on your third marriage and can't understand why things aren't working out again. You still can't believe you worked like a dog to get your first husband through medical school and then he left you for that nurse. And the other husbands weren't much different. You were never in a financial situation where you felt you could take time off work and raise children, so you never had any. You didn't built a high-earning career because you were busy taking care of your spouses.

PROJECT: HEALTH REMODEL
You're a high school teacher and absolutely love it. You never feel more at home than when you're in your classroom, which is full of your handmade posters, creative art pieces, and photographs you've personally taken. The kids love you and you always go the extra mile to make sure your students are successful. You give handmade ornaments to each student for Christmas. Yet you got back from your annual doctor's appointment and have been informed that you have deterioration of the disks in your lower back, high cholesterol, and have been advised to lose fifty pounds.

PROJECT: CAREER REMODEL
You're a college student who's barely making the grades to keep you in school this semester. You can't get out of bed and your roommates have taken to calling you "lazy-smazy." You got your

second MIP (minor in possession charge) from the cops when you were leaving a party on campus the other night. And to top it off, you lost your job at the sandwich shop because you were late for the fifth time in a row.

5 LIFE PATH: The Freedom Seeker
Personal Mission: To Develop Freedom and Discipline in Every Aspect of Your Life

FREEDOM. FUN. FEARLESSNESS. ADVENTURE. All in capital letters! This vibration contains a lot of intense energy and so you have an intense life. You insist on variety and get bored easily. In fact, you need and seek constant stimulation. Escape is the name of your game. You love passion and are here to experience the raw physicality of life on Earth in every way, shape, and form you can muster. Your desire for experience manifests itself in many different ways, through all the sensual and tactile experiences you can grab hold of.

Your life is all about the senses. You long to experience everything in its fullest degree. Things must taste right, smell good, look pretty, and feel pleasing or you're just not happy. You like to look attractive and so you invest time and money in your appearance. If you aren't making use of your high energy and drive, life can easily turn into a soap opera. You're the Drama Queen or Drama King, whipping up excitement wherever you go.

If you're a 5 Path male, you might decide against marrying young, yet if you do, you'll probably get married more than once. If you're a 5 Path female, you can't stand a clingy partner. "Do not control me" is your mantra. A 5 Path needs a lot of space and freedom, especially early in life.

You're likely to be entrepreneurial and would rather not be subject to someone else's authority. There's a wild side to you because you'd truly rather be dead than bored. Your threshold for what you consider boring is pretty low. You also may escape in TV, movies, and books if you don't feel that your actual life is up to your high-drama standards.

You just can't stand still, and often feel restless. Since you're all about sensual pleasures, you can be quick to jump in and out of relationships and can be lured away by the promise of more passion, sex, and excitement elsewhere. Deep down you're probably not interested in commitment, or at least not until you have burned through some years of high intensity and sensual exploration.

What you need to know is that you basically operate *without a filter*. Other people don't experience life with the same emotional intensity you do and it may take you a while to fully understand this distinction. You experience everything in a big way and in what I call "ADHD time." By this I mean that you have all sorts of information swirling around you all of the time and you find it difficult to choose a focal point. You feel you must experience little tidbits of *all* of it. It's like you're a little kid who won't go to sleep at night when your parents have company over for the evening because you're afraid you'll miss out on something.

Your job is to develop self-discipline and routine in your life so that you have a container for your boundless energy and for the information you're taking in. If you don't establish discipline, routine, and a focused sense of purpose, your life will be entirely too chaotic and out of control.

You relish sensual and earthy pleasures. Yet, if you become enmeshed in seeking constant sensual stimulation, you could find yourself struggling with addictions. Be aware that your desire for fun, adventure, sensual pleasure, and escape will draw you into seeking "highs," whether you gain peak experiences through sex, food, drugs, alcohol, travel, or overwork. Any addictive behavior that feels initially comforting to you will most likely become problematic later.

The downside to your experience might be that you become engulfed by fear and turn into the "anti-adventurer," seeking solace in drudgery, paranoia, hyper-sensitivity, overeating (or under-eating), and victimization. Sorry to say, these compulsions are strong when you're on the 5 Life Path.

Your optimal life doesn't consist of sitting around the office and playing video games on the weekends. Expansion, fearlessness, and change are your key values. When you shut down those aspects of yourself, you start to deteriorate and your life becomes smaller and smaller. You might lose your job and take more than a year to find another one. Even if you feel frantic about your bleak financial situation you may not be willing to get out there, shake it up, and do things differently. If you begin working from home, you might become reclusive and have difficulty garnering the courage or energy even to step out of the house to run errands or buy groceries.

If you find yourself resisting the major components of your Life Path vibration, you'll experience depression, anxiety, and frustration galore, and you won't be living your optimal life. If you can take your powerful energy and intentions into a framework, then you'll create a wonderfully productive, satisfying, and exciting life for yourself.

Well-known 5 Life Paths are never boring, never predictable, and always interesting. Two wild and crazy 5 Life Paths whom audiences are fascinated by and love to watch are the late John Belushi (born January 24, 1951) and Mick Jagger (born July 26, 1943). These men are perfect examples of the "you can't reign me in" energy of the 5 vibration.

Then there are the "freedom at all costs" 5 Life Paths, among them the late Malcolm X (born May 19,1925) and the late Adolf Hitler (born April 20, 1889). Notice how I didn't say "freedom for *everyone* at all costs." Both of these men were dynamic individuals who delivered their fiery messages with such conviction that they changed the course of human history. Pretty powerful stuff.

Other well-known 5 Life Paths include Selena Gomez (born July 22, 1992), Ellen DeGeneres (born January 26, 1958), Mark Zuckerberg (born May 14, 1984), Angelina Jolie (born June 4, 1975), and Beyoncé Knowles (born September 4, 1981).

Common threads when a 5 Life Path is working with optimal energies are fearlessness, adventurousness, self-discipline, and the ability to show others how to live their lives fearlessly.

Your life purpose is to find inner freedom through discipline, focus, and depth of experience.

5 LIFE PATH: Potential Challenges

Your potential challenges are:

- To embrace that you're here to find inner freedom through discipline, focus, and depth of experience. You tend to swing between extreme levels of dependence and independence.
- To acknowledge that you feel bored quickly, to recognize that as soon as you begin to feel bored, this is your message that you're *just starting to get the hang of it.*
- To focus on the *depth* of experience rather than the *breadth* of experience. You can be a jack-of-all-trades and still a master of none. What you must realize is that if you truly lend your discipline and focus to one thing you feel passionate about, other experiences and knowledge will magically fall into place right behind it to support you.
- To beware of degenerating from simple self-indulgence to extreme independence in doing what you want whenever you want to the point that your actions are detrimental to your

overall life (such as excessive drug use, being unable to earn an income because of your volatility, and so forth).

- To understand that you often respond to people and situations by being reactive rather than even tempered. Yours is a dramatic path; you often create drama to keep you distracted from creating successful outcomes in your personal and professional life.

- To work through a fear of being tied down by anyone or anything by subconsciously creating issues to work through in the area of *freedom* by involving yourself in a family (or with an individual) who restrict—or seems to restrict—your independence. Often you give your freedom away and then spend a lot of energy being resentful about it and wondering where it went!

- To realize that out of insecurity you tend to manipulate and control others, usually by getting angry or withdrawing. Or you try too hard to please others and later resent them for your own inability to find a productive happy medium. Until you take full responsibility for your own life, you may appear to be a victim, yet you're really a volunteer.

- To face up to the fact that freedom and responsibility go together, as do freedom and discipline. While it's hard for you to hear, the only one standing in your way is *you*.

- To engage in regular cross-training exercise and a consistent, balanced diet. If you don't stick to this routine you could burn out your adrenal system.

- To learn to set priorities is a key for you. You'll be challenged to let go of one thing so that you can focus on another.

- To step back before you subconsciously engage in some form of limitation, including injuries, smothering partners or family members, financial pressures, obesity, anorexia, addiction, or even imprisonment.

- You're quick thinking, energetic, and versatile, despite your tendency to become obsessively focused or, on the flipside, totally scattered. Your greatest challenges aren't external, but internal ones. The strengths you need to develop are largely internal, too. Given to negative thought processes, you can feel imprisoned by your own fears and doubts. So settle down and clear away your distractions. You're not missing anything by paring down your choices; you're actually allowing yourself to fully engage rather than becoming depressed, emotionally paralyzed, or manic.

5 LIFE PATH: Strengths to Develop

- Many 5 Life Paths are "late bloomers." You may take longer to become confident due to sensitivity, fear, and self-doubt. Yet when you do, watch out world! You're unstoppable.

- There's nothing subtle about you. Everything you do is dramatic so you often take the "all or nothing" route. Reign in your energy and you'll find that you're still the most dynamic person in the room.

- You're the life of the party. You can't find freedom in isolation. You need to work through issues of cooperation with yourself and with others. You thrive when interacting with other people. You have so many talents and so much energy that often your focus gets scattered. Place parameters around your goals and your focused energy will get you exactly where you want to go.

- You're a natural salesperson. You can sell anything to anyone as long as you feel it's a great product or service.

- You're really fun. People love to be around you because you always have something funny or interesting to say. You have a great sense of humor and a gift at making people want to get to know you.

- I think of the 5 Life Path this way: It's like you start out as a fully fueled airplane. You can't help but go fast and hard, doing aerobatics like a Blue Angel. You fly like the wind until the middle portion of your life, when you've burned off some fuel and begin to maintain a steadier flight path. You never stop flying; you only become more grounded and disciplined after you've "been there, done that" and begin to crave a sense of stability.

5 LIFE PATH: You Know You Need to Redesign Your Life If . . .
If you can identify with the core issues presented in these examples, knowing the key attributes of your 5 Life Path will help you identify your patterns and offer you some satisfying alternatives.

PROJECT: SPIRITUALITY AND RELATIONSHIP RENOVATION
You've grown up believing that homosexuality is wrong and sinful. You've started a high-profile job and have been highly successful. You just celebrated your twenty-eighth birthday and suddenly you realize that you're gay.

PROJECT: HEALTH REDECORATION OR REMODEL
You can't seem to schedule a time to workout and it's taking a toll on you. You've gained a little weight. You're a vegetarian and yet you don't eat consistently or well (honestly, most days you forget to eat anything until later in the evening).

PROJECT: HEALTH, SPIRITUALITY, CAREER, AND RELATIONSHIP RENOVATION
You can never remember a time when you didn't feel scared. You're afraid of so many things that you have difficulty keeping it together. You don't have many successful relationships because you're afraid of commitment and intimacy. You don't like to travel because of the germs and the possibility of the airplane crashing.

It takes you forever to get out the door to an appointment or any outside activity. You don't sleep well and you're eating habits are questionable. Overall, you can find every reason or excuse not to change anything about the way you're living your life.

6 LIFE PATH: The Nurturer

Personal Mission: To Develop Vision and Acceptance in Every Aspect of Your Life

A person with a 6 Life Path is a natural nurturer, visionary, and champion of justice. You lean toward love and marriage like the proverbial "horse and carriage." If you choose not to be a parent, you'll parent in other ways: with pets, co-workers, and friends. There's a distinct nurturing quality to you, which is coupled with a heightened sense of responsibility.

Have you ever noticed that people are drawn to you, almost as if you're a magnet? Do people come to you with their problems and ask for your help? Do people place you in positions of responsibility even though you don't ask for it? These are all aspects of your vibration that you need to get used to, and embrace. If you dislike being "the responsible one," you'll live a life of frustration and resentment. Knowing that more responsibility will be thrown your way allows you to utilize your innate skills and talents in these areas with a compassionate heart.

You're brilliantly creative and must find ways to use your creativity constructively. If you don't stay busy, you can get caught up in petty things. Because you believe so strongly in the family unit, if happily married, you'd rather spend time with your spouse than with friends. If you're single, you'll establish family dynamics in whatever you do.

If you're a 6 Path woman—especially if you don't have children—you'll tend to attract men who act like little boys. If you're a 6 Path woman and divorced, here's your red flag: You could throw yourself into the lives of your children and have difficulty seeing them as grownups. This isn't healthy for you or for your children. If you're a 6 Path man, your tendency is to attract women who are "damsels in distress" and then you'll wonder why you're again the responsible party in the relationship. In any event, domestic tranquility is actually the goal for you, no matter what you're doing.

You'll prefer to manage or own your own business, since you find it hard to work for others. You also have trouble taking advice or instruction from others.

Another major element of the 6 Life Path is being visionary. You're a magnetic and probably physically attractive person who sees the world in an ideal sense. You have a gift of seeing the bigger picture and can't understand why others can't.

Given your visionary qualities, you're also a perfectionist. You have a tendency to put people on a pedestal and then feel betrayed or disappointed when you discover that they're only human after all. When you're feeling unappreciated, undervalued, or overwhelmed, your tendency is to feel self-righteous, lofty, and superior to everyone else, and you make no bones about communicating this to those around you. You wonder why everyone can't be like you and feel everyone else is "wrong" because they don't believe the same things you do or behave in the same manner as you.

You're a connoisseur of beauty. You seek to beautify the world in whatever fashion you can. Many 6 Life Paths are drawn to careers in the beauty industry, including the fields of makeup, hairdressing, and interior design.

One of your greatest talents is your ability to make others feel guilty or unworthy. The irony here is that deep down you feel this way yourself, so you're your own worst critic.

When you're unhappy, no one in the room is happy. When you're feeling down, you can put up a wall that is cold and punishing. Not to mention that you always have an opinion and are overeager to share it with everyone.

You're an "If you want something done right you just have to do it yourself" kind of person. You want to feel indispensible and then resent being indispensible, even though you're the one who set it up that way. The bottom line is that you're working optimally when you're seeing the perfection in everyone and everything at whatever juncture they're in with their own process. That includes you. When you let go of the "should" and instead rely on your wonderful sense of nurturing, compassion, and service, you'll be the most content.

There are many dimensions to the 6 Life Path. Perhaps you can see yourself in the reflection of the late John Lennon (born October 9, 1940), a 6 Life Path who certainly was magnetic and used his musical talents to work for peace. Other well-known 6 Life Paths include child singer Jackie Evanko (born April 9, 2000), Justin Timberlake (born January 31, 1981), and Britney Spears (born December 2, 1981).

Common threads when a 6 Life Path is "on fire" and working with optimal energies are being reasonably responsible and capable of allowing others their own journeys without judging and criticizing them, allowing for personal imperfections, being nurturing, and trusting in a personal vision of the "big picture."

Your life purpose is to reconcile your high ideals with practical reality and to accept yourself, the world, and the present moment by embracing the perfection of all the apparent imperfection.

6 Life Path: Potential Challenges
Your potential challenges are:
- To understand that you're a visionary with idealistic expectations. These expectations can come at a cost when they aren't grounded in reality.

88

- To get a grip on your perfectionism. You can overcome perfectionist tendencies by remembering the bigger picture rather than obsessing over small details.
- To work against your tendency to lack perspective and patience. When you measure yourself and others against lofty standards, you set yourself and them up for failure.
- To accept yourself and others joyfully. Acceptance leads to a less stressful life. Because your tendency is to stubbornly reject anything that falls short of your high standards—which is almost everything—it's easy for you to become sad, angry, or disheartened.
- To comprehend that you see the world as either perfect or flawed and that you often feel a great sense of disappointment about people in your life and the state of the world around you.
- To see that living with you can be difficult because, in your eyes, no one (including your spouse, children, parents, colleagues, and friends) is ever quite good enough.
- To see that although many times you suppress your judgments with a "live and let live" attitude, those judgments still exist underneath and will eventually need to be dealt with. Mostly you're busy judging yourself and trying to be a good person.
- To be aware that you can live in emotional denial. Often you don't know how you really feel because you focus so hard mentally on what you *should* feel in some ideal sense. Then you convince yourself that you actually feel that way, even though this emotional expression is not a reflection of your true feelings.
- To overcome your habit of incessantly comparing yourself with others. Even though you fear comparison, you can't help but constantly compare yourself to others.
- To beware taking on too much responsibility. This leads to codependence, overprotection, dominating behavior, and

acting like a martyr at work and in relationships.

- To learn to detach. As a natural nurturer, you tend to focus on family. Where this can be unhealthy is if it leads to meddling, interfering, judging, and demanding, "My way or no way."
- You judge yourself harshly and are acutely sensitive to being judged by others. A leap in your development happens when you stop comparing yourself with others. That single shift can create a quantum leap in the way you experience your life.

6 LIFE PATH: Strengths to Develop

- You're a practical idealist. When you find a way to follow your heart and develop patience, you can incrementally share your higher vision, allowing others to evolve at their own pace, not at the pace you dictate. This allows you the most satisfaction in your life.
- You expect high levels of performance from yourself and from others. You have such high standards for yourself that it's a good idea to make it a priority to get back in touch with your authentic self. You could wake up one day with virtually no idea who you really are unless you take the time to get to know yourself—flaws and all.
- You're an amazing boss and excel at business. Your only stumbling block is how you can develop money issues from waiting forever for something (your product, system of management, whatever *it* is) to be so perfect that it never happens. Understand that mistakes made during your process are steps on your ladder of ultimate success.

6 LIFE PATH: You Know You Need to Redesign Your Life If . . .

If you can identify with the core issues presented in these examples, knowing the key attributes of your 6 Life Path will help you identify your patterns and offer you some satisfying alternatives.

PROJECT: RELATIONSHIP REDECORATION OR REMODEL

You run your own business and love your employees. Your employees are loyal and come to you for outside advice on everything from the best gift choice for their son's birthday to problems with another employee. Even though you thrive in your work environment, you're finding that you're operating with a short fuse lately because you feel that everyone is counting on you to take all the responsibility for everything and you just can't understand why you have to do it all yourself. It's to the point that you're coming to work in a bad mood every day.

PROJECT: RELATIONSHIP, HEALTH, AND SPIRITUALITY REMODEL OR RENOVATION

You're a successful hair stylist. You adore making people more beautiful and have a real knack for knowing what will make a person's hair, makeup, and wardrobe shine. You're really close to your family and yet can't seem to find a lasting intimate relationship. You've been engaged several times and yet each relationship ended. You've reluctantly admitted to having an alcohol problem and know that your former fiancé drank a lot, too.

PROJECT: CAREER AND SPIRITUALITY RENOVATION

You're heading toward your fifty-seventh birthday and you're feeling really restless. You've gotten involved in the political landscape in your town and are particularly drawn to working for the cause of organic and non-GMO food production. You've done well financially and you think it's time to retire and take on a leadership role in the local food debates. In fact, you've come up with a great idea for a non-profit organization and for the past few weeks have been up late into the evenings working on a business plan.

7 LIFE PATH: The Seeker

Personal Mission: To Develop Trust and Openness in Every Aspect of Your Life

You were born to learn to have faith in yourself and in others. There is a lot of spiritual energy surrounding you, so you need a strong spiritual base. You would excel as a philosopher, analyst, or researcher because you're always seeking truth and knowledge, and love delving into life's mysteries. You tend to devour information and excel when you're able to consolidate meaning out of a stack of data and then share your findings with like-minded people.

Do you feel as though you're a little out of place in the world? Many 7 Life Paths feel as though they're old souls who are here exploring the material world. You're bright, intelligent, and intense. You're good with technical problems, at writing, and in discovering things.

Do you feel intuitive? You have a natural intuitive ability that is in some ways at odds with your highly analytic mind. This can be a point of confusion for you. On one hand, you're all about data, knowledge, and research, and you need accepted systems of thought to operate in your chosen realm. On the other hand, you're constantly receiving intuitive data that you can't qualify or quantify and it may scare you.

Either you block and suppress your intuition—which could lead to dissatisfaction and ill health—or you learn to respect and balance both aspects of your highly calibrated mind. Perhaps you experience the opposite: You fully embrace your psychic awareness and refuse to use your grounded, analytical abilities. Either way, inviting both aspects of your cognition (analysis and intuition) to co-exist and co-create can have a profoundly positive impact on your life.

Because of the push-and-pull between your belief in hard data and your intuition, it's important for you to take time alone periodically to regroup. Meditation is imperative. Nature is rejuvenating.

You flourish and relax when you connect with the environment in some way. You need consistent exercise to move your energy around as well. Self-care is necessary for you to have a balanced life. You work best in a position where you can spend some time alone.

In healthy, loving relationships, you tend to be honest, loyal, and direct. Even so, you often have trouble being supportive or praising your partner. This behavior is based on a fear that your loved ones might realize you're not "good enough" for them and will leave you. The irony is that if people do leave it's because they feel undervalued and neglected.

In terms of relating: You can have a sharp tongue, so you need to think about your style of communication and the goals you have for communicating. You tend to get stuck in your head. You'll overanalyze everything and every situation. You're also not always the best at understanding people's wants and needs.

You have an air of secrecy about you and enjoy a sense of mystery. You need space and privacy and don't allow others into your personal life unless you invite them in. You may appear aloof to others, yet you are simply observing the world and processing it in your own way. If you don't operate with the higher-level vibration the 7 Life Path Number brings with it, then you're probably exhausting to be around because you will focus on petty things and can appear to be somewhat shallow.

In some ways, it's as if you're visiting the planet because you really don't feel as though you're from here. If you lack the anchor of solid spiritual beliefs, you'll attempt to escape the rather mundane routine of daily life. When you're off track and lack psychospiritual resources, you're drawn to drugs, alcohol, sex, excessive travel, or overwork. You have profound gifts to share with the world. Powerful intuition, refinement, science, and philosophy are your strengths in a lifetime optimally devoted to study and inner reflection.

We love many well-known 7 Life Paths for their mysterious, vulnerable, and complex personas. Given that the 7 Life Path is continuously working with issues relating to trust and openness, no wonder we are fascinated with you—you're so hard to figure out. Johnny Depp (born June 9, 1963) is a perfect example. He has a rather untouchable, yet emotion filled on-screen personality. It always feels as though he's withholding some major piece of information or just needs the right person to help him open up. The same quality is found in the performances of the late Marilyn Monroe (born June 1, 1926), the sex kitten who wanted to be so much more. Her sense of vulnerability made her audience adore and idolize her.

Other notable 7 Life Paths you might relate to include the actresses Mila Kunis (born August 14, 1983) and Julia Roberts (born October 28, 1967), and spiritual teacher Byron Katie (born December 6, 1942).

Common threads when a 7 Life Path is working with optimal energies are being attuned equally to intuition and intellect, wisdom, being at peace with yourself, and not being afraid of opening up emotionally to others.

Your life purpose is to trust yourself, trust others, and trust in the process of your life so that you can feel safe enough to open up and share your inner beauty with the world.

7 LIFE PATH: Potential Challenges

Your potential challenges are:

- To trust and be open. Trust begins with self-trust, which doesn't come easily for you. You often trust your thinking mind over your inner knowing. You need to be open to both forms of knowing.
- To develop your own approach to life. You tend to trust the

views and ideas of others more than your own, so you often attempt to fit yourself to their approaches.

- To evaluate the experts, books, and methods you learn about, embrace that which works best, and listen to your own instincts rather than taking all the information at face value.

- To honor your need for privacy. If you learn to balance your need for private time with your need for social interaction, you will feel more fulfilled.

- To come to terms with your feelings about past betrayals and instances of being misunderstood. The pain you feel has been compounded by the fact that you started out trusting and set yourself up for being misunderstood or taken advantage of.

- To overcome your mixed feelings about intimate relationships. You want them, but you don't. In relationships you need and want a partner for companionship in order to feel a sense of completion, harmony, and balance. You can only have a balanced and healthy intimate relationship when you don't look for completion through another.

- To realize you'll feel most satisfied when you're able to balance your intuition and your analytical mind. You'll be challenged with balancing the two arenas (right brain/left brain).

- To deeply connect with your path of seeking deeper truths. If you fear the unknown, you'll experience a sense of anxiety, confusion, or frustration.

7 LIFE PATH: Strengths to Develop

- You're wise beyond your years. Learning to cultivate and embrace wisdom is your life's purpose. You will learn more effectively through having direct experiences and trial and error experimentation than through reading books or being told.

- You're incredibly intuitive. In order to find your authentic self, focus on cultivating your intuition, knowledge, and acceptance. Having a tendency to lack healthy personal boundaries, you typically share everything you think and feel, and then later feel hurt, betrayed, or misunderstood when people don't respond well to your sharing.

- You're an excellent communicator. Take the opportunity to express yourself directly and openly. When you come to trust yourself and your heart, you've got nothing to fear. When you trust your intuition, you're an insightful guide for others. At the end of the day, you're meant to be a spiritual teacher to yourself and others, in whatever unique manner this teaching manifests for you.

- You're intelligent. You have a highly developed mind and so you also need an equally developed physical body. You need physical exercise, meditation, and time spent in nature. Good outlets for you would be hiking, dance, and martial arts.

- You have high expectations of yourself and others. Keep reviewing your expectations, allowing others (as much as yourself) their journey. This runs the gambit from letting go of your impatience with bad drivers to forgiving someone for having deeply hurt you.

7 LIFE PATH: You Know You Need to Redesign Your Life If . . .
If you can identify with the core issues presented in these examples, knowing the key attributes of your 7 Life Path will help you identify your patterns and offer you some satisfying alternatives.

PROJECT: RELATIONSHIP AND SPIRITUALITY RENOVATION OR REMODEL
You left your husband because you discovered he was cheating on you. Ever since, you've been on a downward spiral. It's been two years since the divorce and yet you can't seem to trust men. You've

dated a little bit, but you always break it off after a few dates, finding good reasons why it won't work out. You've started smoking again. You're just not feeling energized or happy.

PROJECT: CAREER REDECORATION OR REMODEL
You've been a fairly successful graphic designer for several years. You enjoy the problem-solving required to complete a successful project. Lately you've been feeling a bit bored and so you're reacting to people and projects at work with some cynicism. Your boss called you into her office the other day and reprimanded you. She relayed to you that a client called and complained that you basically tore their product line apart at the production meeting yesterday when you were supposed to be reinventing their package design.

PROJECT: CAREER REMODEL
You work as a psychic and, while you're excellent at your job, you just aren't making enough money to support yourself because you can't be bothered with learning about the financial end of doing business. You keep giving away your services and haven't invested the time or money in creating a website or any other kind of marketing.

8 LIFE PATH: The Powerhouse
Personal Mission: To Develop Abundance and Power in Every Aspect of Your Life
The lesson of the 8 Life Path is how to manage your personal relationship with power and money. This path is about establishing and building financial security. You seek the *freedom* that comes from being financially stable. From early on, your drive will center on money in one way or another.

The 8 Life Path isn't particularly easy sailing, since you're meant to use power, influence, authority, and control to make a positive difference in the world. You'll tend to be either a huge success or a major failure—or both at different times. Yours is the journey of money, power, and authority, and, while that may sound fabulous, this path demands a great deal of discipline, wisdom, and fortitude.

Once you accept that yours is a life meant for success and achievement, the real work begins. You've got excellent executive and entrepreneurial skills. A key for you is to think big and find the right processes and people to support you in your enterprises. Focusing intently on your higher purpose will keep you out of trouble—or at least might deter you from getting in a whole heap of trouble.

The 8 Life Path is fairly unforgiving: You don't get away with much. If you're driving five miles over the speed limit surrounded by ten other cars doing the same thing, you're the one who'll get a ticket. It may not seem fair, but that's the way it is.

Martha Stewart (born August 3, 1941) is on an 8 Life Path and her story provides a perfect example. How many other people engaged in the same type of insider trading as Martha Stewart? Yet she's the one who was arrested, tried, convicted, and went to prison. Right or wrong, the 8 Life Path person must act with uncompromising ethics at all times. Martha Stewart bounced right back—*resilience* is another 8 Life Path trait, so take note of it—yet the message is clear: Your ethics will be tested.

You're easily misinterpreted by others, so must learn to be tactful in your communication. You feel compelled to tell "the truth" without padding and that doesn't go well with most people. You see things in a black-and-white manner with little room for gray. You may be the classic workaholic, which partly comes from wanting to be a great provider.

Like the 4 Life Path, the 8 Life Path is rife with family issues. Understand that you've endured some profound experiences in your life, and either you can be ground up and spit out by them or you can choose to see them as your favorite teachers—that they were hard on you gave you the opportunity to learn about yourself.

Strife and struggle can be used to your advantage because through them you'll develop a thick skin for discomfort and also some great skills and tools to help you obtain your goals. One thing you have trouble getting past in your personal life is infidelity. You simply can't get over it and won't be able to forgive, so it's best to let that person go. This also goes for betrayal in business. As an 8 Life Path, be aware that you won't be able to revive the trust you need to make the relationship whole and optimally functional again.

You don't have a lot of tolerance for people who feel sorry for themselves, which is ironic because oftentimes 8 Life Paths view themselves as victims. If you choose to dwell on the negative—and the 8 Life Path typically sees more than its share of what can certainly be considered "negative" —this leads you to deep depression.

A caution: 8 Life Paths often have reoccurring health issues because of stress and addiction. You're also accident prone because sometimes you don't live in the moment and aren't paying attention.

Interestingly, being on the 8 Life Path, with its emphasis on money and power, is no guarantee that you'll live a charmed financial life. An 8 Path person is just as likely to be drawn toward scarcity. You could end up destitute at worst and just "making ends meet" at best. If you can, however, embrace the idea that making money is all right—and for you, not only all right, but imperative to your life purpose—you'll discover it doesn't take much to launch into huge success. The 8 vibration provides the energy with which to achieve financial abundance through concerted effort, ethical conduct, and attention to your higher purpose.

I know many 8 Life Paths who have struggled with a load of issues from childhood who have either succumbed to addiction and victimization or blazed through their fear and anger over their circumstances to rise from the ashes like the Phoenix. That's how dramatic the 8 Life Path can be. I know many 8 Life Paths who've been like the poster child for "The Rise and Fall and Rise of [insert your name here]." They are destitute, addicted, lazy, and then, through some strange turn of events, clean and sober, passionate about *something*, and a millionaire within a year. No kidding.

As an 8 Life Path, take heart. It's not willy-nilly or random chance that you find yourself in the trenches over and over again. The tough stuff is the core of this vibration, making the ultimate rewards you get for your efforts even sweeter.

I already mentioned Martha Stewart. I bring her up again with the intent to illustrate the resilient qualities of the 8 Life Path. You're positioned to bounce back from adversity when you stay positive and keep your ethics clean. How many people could go from being America's cooking and homemaking expert to convict and back again without much tarnish? Lesser folks would have slunk away from the spotlight with their tails between their legs. Not Martha. She's focused on her strengths and goes with it.

The late Paul Newman (born January 26, 1925) was another versatile 8 Life Path whose life history reads like a page-turner. Acting, race car driving, politics, two marriages, children, entre-preneurship, and philanthropy: Newman did it all. He found his way through obstacles to find and act on his passions, embracing the money, power, and authority he cultivated along the way.

A few other 8 Life Paths you might identify with include model and spokesperson Brooke Burke-Charvet (born September 8, 1971), the late singer-songwriter Amy Winehouse (born September 14, 1983), and actress and producer Sandra Bullock (born July 26, 1964).

Common threads when an 8 Life Path is "on fire" and working with optimal energies are being at ease with financial abundance, using power and authority wisely and for the good of others, not dwelling in the negative or becoming a victim to circumstances, and being abundantly giving of time, money, and influence to make the world a better place.

Your life purpose is to use your abundance and power to make the world a better place.

8 LIFE PATH: Potential Challenges

Your potential challenges are:

- To work through issues related to money, power, authority, control, and recognition.
- To reflect and ask: "Do I either strive for control and power or do I give it away?" You may aim to control others around you or give your power away to others who abuse it and you. You might have an authoritarian mate or an abusive parent. You often allow employers, parents, or others treat you with a lack of respect or with contempt until you learn to stand up for yourself and claim your power.
- To work against your impulse to avoid material success. If you don't learn to avoid these impulses, you may end up destitute at worst or just punching the time clock at best. The drive toward material abundance comes with equally strong fears of abundance. Meaning, many times an 8 Life Path will want money and yet because of a belief that money is "evil" or because of negative messages received during childhood, you're challenged by your tendencies to go the opposite direction toward scarcity.
- To understand that issues with money will be likely to recur throughout your life. You may also confront issues of power,

control, authority, or recognition. You may have no issues with money; your major issues may be with power and recognition.

- To embrace the fact that money and spirituality can co-exist.
- To make the leap from self-centered entitlement into giving, generosity, and feelings of abundance, if you were born with a "silver spoon" in your mouth. Those born into wealth have the tendency to distance themselves from other people. If you were born into poverty you may have a tendency to use your history as a rationale for never taking reasonable steps to become financially abundant.
- To make a concerted effort to avoid greed. If you misuse or repress your power, it'll turn around and destroy you. Clarity of focus teamed with a higher purpose is imperative to your healthy success. The central work for you involves contacting your sense of inner abundance, not just striving for material wealth in the outer world.

8 LIFE PATH: Strengths to Develop

- You're a powerful person. You need to experience inner abundance, power, and respect before you can effectively manifest these qualities in the world. Your destiny involves money one way or another. Yet you aren't here just for money; you're here to manifest *abundance* in terms of *attitude* and *feeling*. Find ways to give to others throughout your life.
- You can be successful with anything you focus on accomplishing. When exploring the energy of the 8 Life Path, you find that you have both an attraction and an aversion to success. It's a struggle. Sometimes you can become lazy and bored with life. Though you may face difficulties, you must learn how to focus on your goal, start it, and follow through with the necessary work to manifest your vision.
- Others may find you intimidating. Even if you aren't vocal or

aggressive, your internal sense of power is undeniable. Even when you can't see it, others can. You have concerns about not allowing others to control you. When you're engaged in using your power constructively, you're working with your optimal energy.

- You're a doer and an achiever. Once you realize that you're meant to have financial success in your life, you can start working with your expansive energy. When you banish the feelings that keep you from achievement, you can think big and play big.
- When you focus on what you want with drive and intensity you can achieve anything. Whatever you want is worth working for.

8 LIFE PATH: You Know You Need to Redesign Your Life If . . .
If you can identify with the core issues presented in these examples, knowing the key attributes of your 8 Life Path will help you identify your patterns and offer you some satisfying alternatives.

PROJECT: CAREER AND RELATIONSHIP RENOVATION
You've led a privileged life: being born in a family with money, receiving a good education, having opportunities to travel. Yet you've also experienced a lot of emotional pain that you keep hidden. Your parents divorced. Your father was addicted to drugs and alcohol, but the family wouldn't acknowledge it. He died young. You've worked in the family business and have been subject to harsh treatment by the patriarch of the family. Now you're at a point where you want to strike out on your own, but you're scared and don't know exactly what to do or how to do it.

PROJECT: SPIRITUALITY AND CAREER RENOVATION
You've been working as a cashier at the convenience store ever since you quit high school. You've been thinking about getting

your GED and going to college, but other expenses keep you from making the change. You're feeling depressed because you want something better for yourself, but you just seem to have a lot of bad luck that keeps you from moving forward.

PROJECT: SPIRITUALITY AND HEALTH RENOVATION
You're a musician in a band and have been having major career success. You're traveling the world and making more money than you ever dreamed you would. You're also living the "rock star" lifestyle and are addicted to drugs and alcohol. You had to postpone one of your concerts for the first time because you landed in the hospital after you passed out backstage.

9 LIFE PATH: The Humanitarian
Personal Mission: To Develop Integrity and Wisdom in Every Aspect of Your Life
The 9 Life Path is the most evolved in numerology and has one of the strongest vibrations because it contains the qualities of all the other numbers. If your belief system supports the idea of reincarnation, you might be relieved to know that the 9 vibration is that of a wise old soul, returning to wrap things up. If you don't believe in reincarnation, you'll still be relieved to know that your life is meant to be expansive and spiritually challenging.

Yours is truly a lifetime to focus fully and completely on letting go and surrendering, and on gaining and acting upon higher spiritual principals, however you define them. You've a strong inclination to follow something you believe in, and you'll pursue this with great ambition and drive. You have an authentic regard for humanity, so your goals usually involve serving others in some way.

One of the strongest characteristics of your 9 Life Path is that you often have issues with your original family. You may have felt unloved or abandoned as a child, or perhaps responsible for your parents. In any event, your attachment to your original family is hard to give up. Unlike the 4 Life Path or the 8 Life Path, your family issues reside more distinctly in enmeshment and co-dependence. You must find a way to maintain healthy personal boundaries with your family and find the courage to leave unhealthy dynamics behind.

Many times the life of a 9 Life Path reads like a script from one of the old television nighttime soap operas *Dallas, Falcon Crest,* or *Dynasty.* Nine Life Paths find themselves involved in the family business or feeling compelled to be overly involved in the lives of their family members.

The key to creating your optimal life is to extract yourself from co-dependent relationships. It'll take a lot of strength and courage, because it'll take a while for you to realize that your family dynamics are neither healthy nor serving you.

When you marry and have your own family, you want nothing less than to be the "perfect parent." When it comes to the family, you can't handle interference. If you have trouble with your partner, you don't want your parents or siblings to get involved. You feel capable of resolving the issue.

You're at your best when you engage your spiritual side and listen to you intuitive inner voice, which is crystal clear when you remove your mental clutter.

A note of caution: You do such a great job at taking care of everybody's business that when you're in trouble or need support, people don't even notice. You must let your guard down and ask for what you need. Your needs aren't easily read by others—you have to ask for help.

When you're in a room, everyone assumes you're in charge. You're a leader in many ways, yet you often place a lot of pressure on yourself. You need to lighten up and forgive yourself for being human.

Many 9 Life Paths don't really feel they belong on the planet, if you know what I mean. You rival the 1 and 7 Life Paths with feelings of not quite belonging. You have an intimidating quality and yet putting others at ease is actually one of your gifts if you cultivate it. You're sometimes accused of being patronizing because you have a tendency to preach rather than being an active listener.

Your life revolves around loss of all kinds, so it can be confusing and disheartening unless you surrender yourself and allow what's next to come into your life with open arms rather than with bitterness. Your story of loss and pain is sometimes overwhelming and can drag you into apathy or resentment.

Your higher purpose is to inspire others with your compassion for humanity. You're in your element when you're inspiring others by your example, not by what you say. You have incredible charisma and can choose to use that in either positive or negative ways. You would make an amazing teacher, counselor, or therapist. You are good with children. You also would do well in a creative field. You would make a wildly successful entrepreneur or businessperson if it's with something you feel wholeheartedly passionate about. You must choose work that has meaning for you or you'll feel lost or empty. When you are optimizing your energy, you're a powerful force for change.

I've found that many 9 Life Paths have an incredible capacity for success with anything they set out to do. Yet I've also found that when a 9 Life Path succumbs to holding on to difficult experiences with a bitter vice-grip, chances are that this individual is hiding out from expanding into the gifts he or she inherently bring to the table as a 9 Life Path.

Remember: You hold the constructive elements of all of the other numbers in numerology, and you hold all of the destructive elements as well. Sound like a big responsibility? It actually is. This responsibility lies deeply within you and in your ability to understand the vastness of your playing field if you come to embrace it.

Your amazing potential reminds me of the 2008 film *The Curious Case of Benjamin Button,* a story in which Benjamin is born an old man in an infant's body. As he matures, he meets himself in the middle of his life and then begins to become younger as time passes. He eventually dies of old age as an infant again.

The key element to take away from Benjamin Button's story is that he flows through his life with awe and appreciation, with a healthy sense of detachment, soaking in all of his experiences in the moment, observing other people, engaging in love, and not clinging to any single part of his multilayered life journey. You can use his story as a primer for creating your own life.

You're certainly at your best when you're moving with the flow rather than ensconced in old stories about the past and replaying old hurtful experiences. It's all a matter of perspective.

The most important advice: Take care not to live in the past. Move forward as you gently release yesterday, live today, and embrace tomorrow.

The late Ray Charles (born September 23, 1930) could very well have become overwhelmed with his circumstances early on and never had the confidence to break through the barriers he was able to break through as a African-American and as a blind musician. In the true spirit of the 9 Life Path, he found his voice in music and gave his gift to millions of people.

Actor/comedian Eddie Izzard (born February 7, 1962) is a 9 Life Path who embodies the vibration. Currently, Izzard has taken to championing humanitarian causes, become politically engaged, and began running marathons to help raise money for causes he feels strongly about, despite the fact that he wasn't a runner when he started participating.

On the undeniably humanitarian end of the 9 Life Path, the late Mother Teresa (born August 26, 1910) exemplified the spirituality of the 9 Life Path vibration. Her life was devoted to serving humanity in every way she could.

More contemporary 9 Life Paths you might identify with include talk show host and actress Ricki Lake (born September 21, 1968) and singer Justin Bieber (born March 1, 1994).

Common threads when an 9 Life Path is "on fire" and working with optimal energies are giving back to the world with gifts and talents, detachment from old family wounds, empathetic listening, and being open to new experiences every day.

Your life purpose is to live in with the highest integrity, to align your life's purpose with your heart's intuitive wisdom, and to inspire others by your example.

9 LIFE PATH: Potential Challenges

Your potential challenges are:

- To embrace that you're meant to lead by example, not by "lip service."
- To recognize that you're amazingly charismatic, so you can lead or mislead. People will follow you anywhere, so make sure you're heading in the right direction.
- To see that you have a tendency to "bend" spiritual laws or ignore higher principles and have difficulty taking responsibility for your actions. This includes habits of "little white lies," embellishment, and withholding information when it's convenient for you.
- To come to terms with your past. Since acknowledging and healing issues in your past is a major part of your life's work, you may find that you dwell in the past and use those experiences to excuse present behavior or place yourself in the position of the "victim."
- To know that you might swing from extremes of righteous moral responsibility to ignoring moral guidelines altogether,

depending on what you feel you need at the time.

- To step back and see that because you can become a fanatic on almost any subject, you allow extremes in thought and action to overtake you.
- To work through family issues. You can have a "rebel without a cause" mentality where you exert control wherever you feel you can for no particular reason. When you decide that your life is truly of your own making and the past doesn't control your future, you'll release yourself from feeling powerless and angry.
- To ensure you don't become lazy or feel entitled. You may not have been required to take full responsibility for your life, especially if you come from a privileged family of origin.

9 LIFE PATH: Strengths to Develop

- You're ambitious. Develop the qualities of ambition, responsibility, and idealism, and then use them to help you take small steps toward your goals.
- You're artistic and creative. You're at your best when you translate the idealistic into the practical. Cultivate avenues where you can see your creative projects come to fruition.
- You're sensitive. If you can release judgments about yourself and other people, you can generate a deep healing in your life. When you truly come to terms with the concept that your life is full of loss and that letting go is a lifelong requirement you'll be at your most powerful.
- You're a giver. You care deeply about other people, animals, and the environment. You're positioned to be a great leader in any humanitarian field. Choose your passion and follow through with enthusiasm without allowing the problems of the world to drag you into pessimism.
- You're a bundle of creative energy and serve yourself best when

you are giving back in some capacity. Make sure you engage in acts of service that feed your feelings of personal empowerment.

- You're passionate. Developing a trusted set of skills to fall back on in a pinch will offer you welcome relief from feelings of unworthiness. Concentrate on your passions and your strengths; leave the other stuff to someone else.

9 LIFE PATH: You Know You Need to Redesign Your Life If...
If you can identify with the core issues presented in these examples, knowing the key attributes of your 9 Life Path will help you identify your patterns and offer you some satisfying alternatives.

PROJECT: CAREER, RELATIONSHIP, AND SPIRITUALITY RENOVATION
You had a promising athletic career ahead of you. You were a semester away from graduating from college and signing with the NFL when you had a car accident that damaged your spine. You've been learning to walk again and are beating the odds, yet you'll never be able to play ball again. You're wondering what's next for you.

PROJECT: RELATIONSHIP REDECORATION OR REMODEL
You were diagnosed with ADHD and dyslexia as a kid, but that didn't stop you from becoming a star in math class. You were the one who always befriended the kid who was the oddball. You've built a solid and satisfying career. You're now in your forties and want to improve your emotional relationships with your kids and spouse. You feel you've been more detached emotionally than you'd like to be and that's putting a strain on your relationships. You started seeing a counselor for the first time to help you understand how to retool the way you relate.

PROJECT: SPIRITUALITY, HEALTH, AND CAREER RENOVATION

You've always been a "rebel without a cause," careening through life erratically. You operate with an all or nothing mentality and often feel frustrated with other people and with yourself. You volley from open-hearted and empathetic to critical and angry. You're heading into your twenty-eighth birthday and want a big change in your life. You can see how you've been standing in your own way and sabotaging your decisions you've been making. You're not satisfied with your sporadic job or with your short-lived intimate relationships, and your health has been suffering.

THREE MASTER PATH NUMBERS

IF YOU FIND AN 11, 22, OR 33 before you digit-down your 2, 4, or 6 Life Path Number (revisit page 52), this means you are journeying on a Master Path. The three Master Path Numbers we'll be looking at are 11/2, 22/4, and 33/6. The key with a Master Path is to remember that you are always given *significant strengths* and *significant challenges*. So while it may sound lofty to be on a "Master" Path, it's going to require more from you.

You might find that the energy of your Master Path Number serves to magnify the inherent challenges, tendencies, and obstacles of your single-digit Life Path Number while pushing you toward a higher sense of purpose. The Master Paths are what I would consider spiritually based; meaning, when you're working optimally with a Master Path vibration you must, in fact, be pursuing a higher spiritual purpose. There's no getting around it.

So when you discover a Master Number in your calculations, take time to reread the section corresponding to the single-digit Life

Path Number (the 2, 4, or 6) that it pertains to, because the Life Path is your primary task at hand. What you'll find is that in order to step into the Master Path, you must raise your own vibration. Doing so always requires paying attention to your spiritual life, however you define it. You'll encounter more intense challenges and obstacles when you're on a Master Life Path. Bottom line: It's not easy.

THE 11/2 MASTER LIFE PATH

Reread the 2 Life Path description (see page 59). To this, add the following insights.

You've the potential for fame with this Master Path. Basically, you're a creative genius capable of the highest forms of artistic expression and the realization of inspired ideas. You can potentially change the consciousness of the world with your artistic gifts when you use them to help others.

Unlike the 22/4 Master Path, which you'll learn is more practical in its application, the 11/2 Master Path is artistic, creative, and inspiring in a rather intangible way. What I mean by that is this: an 11/2 Master Path might create a piece of art, a dance, a performance piece, music, or a sculpture that affects the viewer in a way that the viewer can't explain. Rather than seeing a tangible result from the contribution or the experience, the 11/2 Master Path's power resides in the inexplicable transformative experience they provide.

Are you pulled toward any kind of applied art, music or dance? Many 11/2 Life Paths are superior musicians or singers. These arts are potential outlets for your Master Path energy.

The 11/2 Master Path means you'll face internal struggles throughout your life. You're the most intuitive, sensitive, and artistic person around, and your feelings get hurt very easily. You'll find that you're challenged with being self-absorbed and do battle with your ego.

You're meant to do great things, yet you can be conflicted. You've always felt different: both superior and inferior. You have a tendency to question your work, feeling as though you need to do more, something different, or something more important. Develop the internal guidance of your intuition and you'll have less difficulty discovering and acting on your true passion.

Remember, although you may garner fame and recognition from your endeavors, attention is often accompanied by criticism. Knowing how sensitive the 2 Life Path is to criticism, you must learn to protect yourself emotionally. Develop a thick skin in order to operate and follow through with your work without having a nervous breakdown. If you succumb to the destructive tendencies that the intense 2 vibration brings, you'll be prevented from accomplishing everything you were born to do.

You might identify with these 11/2 Master Paths: Steven Colbert (born May 13, 1964), Jennifer Aniston (born February 11, 1969), Robert Downey, Jr. (born April 4, 1965), and Bill Clinton (born August 19, 1946).

11/2 MASTER PATH: You Know You Need to Redesign Your Life If...

If you can identify with the core issues presented in these examples, knowing the key attributes of your 11/2 Life Path will help you identify your patterns and offer you some satisfying alternatives.

PROJECT: SPIRITUALITY, RELATIONSHIP, AND HEALTH RENOVATION

You were addicted to drugs and alcohol from your teens into your thirties. It took losing your job, your wife, and custody of your kids to wake you up. You've been in rehab for a month and are beginning to plan for your future.

113

PROJECT: RELATIONSHIP DECORATION

You're a successful web developer who has been happily married for ten years and you have two beautiful children whom you adore. Your husband has been talking about how much he misses hearing you sing, because you gave that up when you got busy raising your kids. You're considering joining a band as their lead singer.

THE 22/4 MASTER LIFE PATH

Reread the description of the 4 Life Path (see page 72). To this, add the following insights.

As a 22/4 Life Path, you're destined for material and financial success when you focus your energy on making a significant, inspired contribution to the way we think and lead our *everyday lives*. You can do this in any way you desire: through business, politics, art, the humanities, or science.

Hard work is at the core of the 22/4 Master Path, so don't shrink from your duty. Your challenge is to locate your passion so you can move forward in manifesting your dreams with confidence. If you're working more in the 4 energy, you'll be exhausted rather than energized.

What this means is that you need to be more inspired and connect to higher ideas. This is a challenge for the 4 energy, which is all about being practical and detail oriented. To engage fully in the 22 energy, you must pull your focus out of the details and into the big picture. Have others provide the support you need to expand your enterprise.

You're constantly seeking order and have a tendency to be a "bulldozer" in your interactions. You've an innate tendency to act on what you "know is right" without concern for those around you, making you challenging to live with or work for.

Surrendering your "staff position" for the CEO's job can bring about a huge adjustment in the ways you think and traditionally operate. You'll be challenged to find the courage to let go of micromanaging the details and move your project, career, or enterprise into the Big Leagues, where it belongs.

You might identify with these 22/4 Master Paths: Tina Fey (born December 2, 1970) and Kim Kardashian (born October 21, 1980).

PROJECT: CAREER REMODEL OR RENOVATION

You've always been a hard worker at everything you do. Recently, you're feeling bored and frustrated with your job. You've been working with this idea for the past year about a product you'd love to design and get on the market, but you don't have enough money and your staff position doesn't allow you much extra time to get your idea off the ground. You're wondering if you should just shelf the idea, but it keeps gnawing at you.

PROJECT: CAREER RENOVATION

As an accountant, you've felt great satisfaction helping people work out their finances. Yet you find that when it comes to your own finances, you just can't take a leap of faith. You still enjoy your job, but lately you've been feeling a pull toward something "bigger," although you're not quite sure what it is. You're passionate about new solar technologies and have been researching how to start your own solar panel company. You're feeling a lot of fear around the idea of abandoning your current job for something so drastically different.

THE 33/6 MASTER LIFE PATH

Reread the description of the 6 Life Path (see page 86). To this, add the following insights.

The mission of your Life Path is to bring a new kind of healing to the world. Yours is the journey of the healer, which can manifest in many different aspects of your life. In whatever you do, you'll be drawn to help, heal, and inspire others. You can do this directly by becoming an intuitive coach, counselor, psychic medium, hands-on healer, or mystic. Or you can use your gifts more subtly in whatever field you choose, from actor to real estate agent.

You're highly artistic. Your destiny (and challenge) is to cultivate your natural, high-minded vision of the bigger picture and support others to reach their own potential.

You're here to learn to use your expressive creative energy in the most constructive and uplifting ways. You'll help others recognize that all of the obstacles and pain they experience is simply fuel for their own growth and learning.

You're in your element when you're working for justice and truth in constructive ways, using your incredible creativity and healing abilities. To succeed, you need to get a grip on your ideals, reign in and focus on a goal, stay practical and realistic, and remain positive, especially in the face of obstacles.

You might identify with these 33/6 Life Paths: Stephen King (born September 21, 1947), Lindsay Lohan (born July 2, 1986), and Charlie Sheen (born September 3, 1965).

PROJECT: RELATIONSHIP REMODEL OR RENOVATION

You've devoted your life to your church. You regularly participate in church activities (including the choir and the women's league) and work as an independent contractor for the local housing placement service. You have five children by four different husbands. You just can't seem to choose the right man; they all end up abusing you. You've just separated from husband number five and you're contemplating what to do next.

PROJECT: HEALTH, SPIRITUALITY, AND RELATIONSHIP RENOVATION

You've always struggled with a condition that was finally diagnosed as bipolar disorder. It's been difficult to have continuity with the relationships in your life because of your volatility and unpredictable behavior. Your family loves you, but they have been clear with you that they won't bail you out of any more messes. You're not sure how to do it, but you know you need to get yourself together—because your whole world is falling apart.

SUMMARY

Your Life Path Number is the first and most important tool in your redesign toolbox.

1 Life Path: Creativity and confidence

2 Life Path: Cooperation and harmony

3 Life Path: Expression and communication

4 Life Path: Process and stability

5 Life Path: Freedom and discipline

6 Life Path: Nurturing and acceptance

7 Life Path: Trust and openness

8 Life Path: Power and abundance

9 Life Path: Integrity and wisdom

11/2 Master Path: Selfless service and artistic creativity

22/4 Master Path: Masterful teaching and inspired practical ideas

33/6 Master Path: Masterful healing and inspired vision

YOUR LIFE PATH NUMBER will be your single most important tool in the process of redecorating, remodeling, or renovating your life. However, now that you know your Life Path Number, it's time for you to add a second important tool to your toolbox: the Personal Year Cycle. Working with Personal Year Numbers is a wonderful way to go along with the flow of your life rather than clash against it.

What Are Personal Year Cycles?

A PERSONAL YEAR CYCLE is a nine-year-long cycle. Depending on where you are in your cycle, your Personal Year Number could be a 1, 2, 3, 4, 5, 6, 7, 8, or a 9. After 9, you'll cycle back to 1 again.

Each Personal Year Number has different qualities to it. You start your life in the same number year as your Life Path Number. So, for example, if you are a 5 Life Path, you start your life during the year you were born, with a 5 Personal Year. Then you continue to cycle through to a 9 Personal Year and begin the sequence again, the calendar year after that, with a 1 Personal Year. Switching Personal Year Numbers happens every year throughout your life.

Keep in mind that the numbers 1–9 vibrate with the same energies and meanings whether they inform your Life Path or your Personal Year Cycle. So if you're familiar with the defining qualities of all the Life Path Numbers, you have an advantage as you learn how the energies of the Personal Year Numbers affect you. These operate in similar ways on a yearly basis.

Have you ever noticed how there are certain times when things feel as if they're happening effortlessly? At such times, life feels so energizing, just so undeniably *right*. And then aren't there other times when everything you do seems like a struggle and life feels downright excruciating? Ever looked for a job for a full year and then—*Bang!* —the perfect one falls into your lap with little effort on your part as soon as the next year rolls around? That's partly because of where you are in your Personal Year Cycle.

Having knowledge of the number of the Personal Year that you're in will help you establish a framework for your activities that responds to the basic energy of that number. Knowing your Personal Year Number will offer you shortcuts for making decisions that can make your life easier, more productive, and ultimately happier. At the very least, knowing your Personal Year Number in a given year offers you an overarching idea about the arena you'll be engaged with during that specific year.

If you realize, for example, that during your 8 Personal Year you will be met with intensified issues related to money and personal power, then you can work with that knowledge during the year rather than resisting or attempting to avoid it. If nothing else, knowing your Personal Year Number has the potential to set you up for making more mindful decisions during each year.

Remember also, when you're in a Personal Year that has the same number as your Life Path Number, you'll feel "double indemnity" from the slings and arrows of the year. What I mean to say is that if, for instance, you are a 2 Life Path and you are in a 2 Personal Year, you're going to feel all the positives doubly. Yet this also means that you're going to be doubly challenged with the destructive tendencies inherent in the year's vibration. Fortunately, knowing this you can protect yourself.

So if you're in a 2 Personal Year and you have a 2 Life Path, the year will be fraught with oversensitivity and lots of opportunities to work on balancing your love and care of others with your own personal self-care. It'll be a year where your psychic boundaries will be put to the test. It may feel excruciatingly slow moving, and you'll need to put absolute attention on the creation of cooperative activities and harmony. By knowing your Personal Year Number, you can consider yourself forewarned of how best to flow with the challenges you'll face.

Can you imagine experiencing a 9 Personal Year as a 9 Life Path? Wow. People with 9 Life Paths experience loss throughout their lives in the first place. Then lay a 9 Personal Year on top of that, a year where loss, letting go, and huge transitions are the key features, and watch out.

The point is: You'll experience intense energies inherent to the strengths, tendencies, and obstacles of your Life Path Number during your Personal Year when the numbers are matching.

Here is how to calculate your Personal Year Number. Add together the month and the day of your birth date. Then, instead of adding the digits of your year of birth to the subtotal (as you did to discover your Life Path Number), add in the digits of the *current year:* For the sake of the following example, let's say the current year is 2012.

EXAMPLE: BIRTH DATE JUNE 22, 1963

6/22/2012

$6 + 2 + 2 + 2 + 0 + 1 + 2 = 15$

$1 + 5 = 6$

Based on this formula, for the Personal Year Cycle that relates to this particular birthday in 2012 you'd be in a 6 Personal Year.

The next section explains the defining qualities to each year in your Personal Year Cycle.

What to Expect During Each Year in Your 1–9 Personal Year Cycle

IN THE SAME WAY that the nine Life Path Numbers have particular energies associated with each of them, so do the nine Personal Year Numbers. Notice that the cycles here reflect the same or very similar core energies to those we relate to the Life Path Numbers. The key principle of life design to think about is this: *Go with the energy of the year.*

If you're in a 7 Personal Year and you're trying to land a new job that'll require lots of travel, heavy client interaction, and little downtime, you might find that you sabotage your chances of getting the job in some way (usually by "not feeling like" putting yourself out there). Or you might apply for it because this is the job you've always wanted and you're highly qualified to do it, yet you don't get chosen for it—and you don't know why.

This is just an example, yet these two experiences are typical of what happens to people in the midst of a 7 Personal Year. During a 7 Personal Year it's best to focus on study and introspection. Simply understand that this new job would have been the opposite of those activities. The energy you find yourself immersed in this year is really not compatible with your immediate goal.

But wait! The next year comes around and somehow that same job is available again. You're now in your 8 Personal Year, a year that's all about the energy of financial abundance and work. You apply to the same human resources office with the same résumé, get a call for an interview, and score the job right then, on the spot. Now they offer you more money than you ever imagined because during the interview you can talk about the series of seminars you attended the preceding year (during your year of study). Not only that, they are also really impressed that you were current on a particular business system you spent your 7 Personal Year studying or that you had interacted with a particular teacher.

The vibration of an 8 Personal Year supports your success in the active, moneymaking realm whereas the 7 vibration *prepares you* for success by making sure you focus inward and gain necessary knowledge, even if you don't understand why you're doing what you're doing.

You'll find that when you're aware of the basic energy surrounding the number of the year you're experiencing, you can work with the flow of the energy rather than against it. Thus, your success rate, and your mental, physical, emotional, and financial health can rise exponentially.

PERSONAL YEAR NUMBER REFERENCE GUIDE

HERE ARE THE DEFINING QUALITIES of each year in the Personal Year Cycle. Use these descriptions as a reference guide to contemplate what happened last year, what's on the docket for this year, and what's coming up next year.

The 1 Personal Year

THIS IS THE BEGINNING of a new Personal Year Cycle. During the previous year (a 9 Personal Year) everything was coming to a conclusion and falling away. This year (a 1 Personal Year) brings new ideas and new energies into perspective. It's time to start taking action in a solid direction. This is your year to lay the foundation for all that is to come in the new cycle. It's a busy year and needs your concerted effort and action to move things forward.

You may be feeling a bit shell-shocked from your prior 9 Personal Year, so be sure to allow yourself sufficient time to recalibrate in this year of beginnings. Even though it'll be a relief to be out of the 9 Personal Year and into the newness of your 1 Personal Year, there can be some residual issues you still have to work through at the beginning of this new year that came up in your 9 Year.

Focus on closure from last year's events even as you look ahead to what you'd like your new nine-year cycle to bring into your life. Ideas will begin to mature and take shape this year. For instance, if you lost your job last year, you might trip into a new position this year, or decide to go back to school, or suddenly realize how to really get that new business off the ground. You get the picture.

If you got a divorce last year, this year you can start to rebuild your life with a sense of being grounded rather than overwhelmed with raw emotion. If you had a baby last year, this is the year where it really begins to sink in that your life has been altered in a big way. This is the time to lay out the "clean sheets" and start this nine-year cycle with conscious focus and direction.

PROJECT REDECORATE

Initiate small changes during the 1 Personal Year, such as reviewing your diet and exercise program, reading the five books you have sitting on your bedside table collecting dust, or get the puppy you're now ready to care for.

PROJECT REMODEL

Take concerted and persistent action during the 1 Personal Year, such as formulating a solid business plan for the new business you want to launch, settling in to your new parenting duties if you recently had a baby, or coming up with some fresh ideas to liven up and renew your relationships.

PROJECT RENOVATE

Cultivate your self-confidence and leadership skills during the 1 Personal Year. Some steps might include finalizing your divorce, making extreme lifestyle changes due to health issues or a crisis, or rebounding and recovering from a death in the family or other trauma.

BENEFITS OF THE 1 PERSONAL YEAR

- You'll feel as though a weight has been lifted from you this year after the intensity of the just-finished 9 Personal Year.
- You'll feel a new sense of clarity about the direction you want to take in your life.
- You'll have renewed energy to move forward.

- You'll have the opportunity to tap into your unique vision for your future.
- You'll feel as though you have a fresh start in your life.

POTENTIAL CHALLENGES DURING THE 1 PERSONAL YEAR

- Be aware that you'll feel as though whatever you're doing, you have to do it all by yourself. There's a feeling of isolation and of having to "go it alone." This is part of the energy of the 1 Personal Year. It's an opportunity to develop mastery over how you're building and creating the next segment of your life.
- Protect yourself from low self-esteem by renewing your skill set and reminding yourself of your successes and the different ways you've continuously overcome adversity.
- Be prepared to default into a confrontational mode so that when you do, you recognize it and move past it quickly. You're being asked to define your identity and follow a unique vision; therefore you'll encounter many tests involving strength and courage.

During a matching 1 Life Path and 1 Personal Year, expect a year of intensity surrounding core issues related to:

- Developing leadership and individuality.
- Developing creativity and confidence.
- Feelings of emotional isolation.
- Being critical and judgmental.
- Feeling the intense need to march to the beat of a different drummer.

The 2 Personal Year

THIS IS A YEAR TO FOCUS on your emotions. Last year = career. This year = love and emotions. Concentrate on intimacy and relationships, fostering appreciation for yourself and your loved ones, and speaking your truth gently, yet firmly. Rediscover how you feel, and fine tune the ways you express your emotions. This is a slow-moving year. Things won't happen with immediacy or at the snap of a finger. You need patience in everything you do this year.

You may feel emotionally tender in a 2 Personal Year. If you don't usually feel emotional, this sensitivity could take you by surprise. If you often feel emotionally sensitive, be prepared for more volatility than you're used to experiencing. It's a year to cultivate a thicker skin when it comes to other people's opinions of you—or should I say of what you *think* other people think of you. It's a year of focusing on whatever you can do to be of service to yourself, your family, and causes you feel strongly about. It's an "us" year rather than a "me" year.

Understand that this is a year devoted to cultivating harmony and balance in all aspects of your life, so you also may be challenged with the inclination to go the opposite direction and get caught up in situations that challenge your sense of fairness. Trust that this is a great year to step back and develop a healthy detachment from overwhelming emotions. Learn to look at life from a level of healthy detachment. It's here that you'll begin to detect where other people are truly coming from (good, bad, or indifferent), and to see that even though you think everything revolves around you, it really doesn't. Isn't that a freeing thought? This is the year to take this lesson to your core: Don't take things personally.

PROJECT REDECORATE

Initiate small steps during the 2 Personal Year. Balance is key. Consider reviewing your communication style and making small adjustments (for instance, are you being too timid or too blunt?), clearing out your closet and letting go of unwanted items, or practicing self-care and anxiety reduction by getting a regular massage.

PROJECT REMODEL

Take concerted and persistent action to come to terms with over-sensitivity during the 2 Personal Year. The energy of this year supports your efforts and offers you ample opportunities to speak up in your personal and professional interactions, learn to compromise without getting your feelings hurt, or learn some new skills that help you feel more confident.

PROJECT RENOVATE

Cultivate your sense of self during the 2 Personal Year. Some steps might include entering into an entirely new profession, getting therapy in order to construct healthy emotional and personal boundaries, or returning to school in order to redirect your life.

BENEFITS OF THE 2 PERSONAL YEAR

- You'll feel empowered as the "go to" person in your professional and personal interactions.
- You'll feel a sense of loving, harmonious energy enveloping you.
- You'll enjoy and have success working with the details in your life.
- You'll have the opportunity to practice a sense of balance as you are given opportunities to see both sides of every story.
- You'll feel unhurried.

CHALLENGES DURING THE 2 PERSONAL YEAR

- Be aware that if you struggle with the destructive aspects of the 2 Personal Year, you'll be faced with issues such as the need to learn and practice tact, to act with sensitivity to others' feelings, and to work out issues related to codependency.
- Protect yourself from basing your actions on what other people think of you by reminding yourself that you can't control other people, you can only control yourself.
- Be prepared to default into an over-generous mode and then withdraw from the situation where you've given with resentment. Get to know your triggers. Learn to recognize when they are presented to you and how to step back and think through your response rather than responding with a "black or white" answer.

During a matching 2 Life Path and 2 Personal Year, expect a year of intensity surrounding core issues related to:

- Developing balance and harmony.
- Developing and using your "psychic shield."
- Feelings of emotional sensitivity.
- Responding with harshness and an aggressive need to be right.
- Difficulty successfully working with others.

The 3 Personal Year

THIS IS A YEAR of fun and creativity. Take center stage. Enroll in a public speaking class or have a makeover. Live your life big and expansively. Take risks you'd usually never dream of taking. This is your year to be *out there*, not hunkered down in your cubicle or at home eating frozen dinners and watching TV. The energy of this year is a welcome respite to the slow and deliberate energies of last year. Enjoy everything that you possibility can. Make and take time for fun, for celebrations, for anything that brings you joy.

This year will challenge you with a restless energy to get up and go. If you're in business, you might feel a burning impulse to recommit to networking with more consistency. Make it a routine. You might feel like taking an acting or pottery class, or joining the writers group you've been thinking about joining for a while now. You'll feel compelled to revisit your eating habits and try out a new exercise regimen.

You may find yourself hosting more parties or get-togethers at home and feel a crazy urge to clean out your closet and give most of your old clothes to Goodwill. This may be the year you get a facial for the first time, take a dance lesson, or finally try out for a part in a community theatre production. If you feel blocked in areas of creative self-expression, this is a perfect year for counseling, body-work, public speaking classes, or any other avenue to get to know your emotional self better.

In between all of these activities, you may feel waves of self-doubt. You may feel a tug-of-war between joy and a strange sense of malaise or depression. Understand that such emotions are only partial aspects of truly embracing this year of creativity and emotional self expression. Let it all flow.

PROJECT REDECORATE

Initiate small changes during the 3 Personal Year, such as taking a writing class, learning how to say "no" to obligations you don't really want to do, or learn to play whatever musical instrument you've been longing to play.

PROJECT REMODEL

Take concerted and persistent action during the 3 Personal Year, such as learning how to follow through on projects, take steps to quell your insecurity or feelings of inadequacy, or make a commitment to strengthen your communication skills in whatever capacity you feel needs it the most.

PROJECT RENOVATE

Cultivate your sense of joy and creativity during the 3 Personal Year. Some steps might include getting your own radio show, committing to a creative project you have had on hold for years, or going back to school.

BENEFITS OF THE 3 PERSONAL YEAR

- You'll feel creative, communicative, and ready to get yourself "out there."
- You'll feel lighter and fun loving.
- You'll feel the impulse to shake things up.
- You'll have the opportunity to tap into your sense of joy.
- You'll feel expansive, as though you have a lot to give to yourself and to the world.

CHALLENGES DURING THE 3 PERSONAL YEAR

- Be aware that you'll feel scattered with all the creative energies around you. Make sure to focus on specific goals and actions or you'll feel like a spinning top.
- Protect yourself from bouts of depression or self-doubt by being aware that those emotions are key players this year. Recognize the signs so you can move through them effectively.
- Be prepared for defaulting into sarcasm or criticism when you are feeling overwhelmed.

During a matching 3 Life Path and 3 Personal Year, expect a year of intensity surrounding core issues of:
- Developing all aspects of creative self-expression.

- Developing a light-hearted approach to life.
- Feelings of emotional sensitivity, depression, inadequacy, and overwhelm.
- Responding with cynicism and sarcasm.
- Juggling extreme mood fluctuations.

The 4 Personal Year

THIS IS A YEAR TO WORK hard and sharpen your skill set. You may be exhausted from the constant action of your previous year, so take the time to slow down, steady your pace, and become more methodical about which goals you want to reach for.

Have you always wanted to put your love and knowledge of bird watching into play? This is the year to start teaching a class at your Audubon Society and sharing your enthusiasm, knowledge, and skills. Want something else? Write down and start implementing a long-term plan for your life.

Yet be realistic. Research the finer points of materializing whatever you want. Don't skip any steps or you'll regret it.

This is a year that feels serious. It's the year to plant seeds and make sure that you're doing everything you can to prepare for future growth. This is also a year where you'll be challenged by old family issues that come to the surface for revisiting and potential healing. This year is filled with hard work and the building of foundations, whether those are geared toward new goals or coming to terms with old wounds.

This is a perfect time to delve into the self-help books and study groups of your choice, depending on your past experiences. Do you come from an alcoholic family? Try an Al-Anon meeting. Experienced abuse as a child? Learn how to overcome your emotional triggers through reading books, attending support groups, going to therapy, or engaging in bodywork. Still grieving over the death of a loved one? It's time to seek help and support to move through those feelings of loss successfully. Any step-by-step approach to identifying and working with family history or trauma is very powerful during a 4 Personal Year.

PROJECT REDECORATE

Initiate small changes during the 4 Personal Year. Control and procrastination are key components this year, so taking measured, manageable steps is the key to success. This year supports your efforts in organizing your home office and cleaning your garage, figuring out small ways to add some oomph to your relationships, or committing yourself to a structured exercise program with an emphasis on stretching and flexibility.

PROJECT REMODEL

Make a concerted effort to come to terms with workaholic tendencies during the 4 Personal Year. Take time to yourself. Enjoy getting out into nature on a regular basis. Spice up your wardrobe. The energy of this year supports your efforts to remain flexible yet focused, learn to use your creativity with projects and relationships, or develop an expansive view about how to get things done.

PROJECT RENOVATE

Cultivate hard work and setting up foundations during the 4 Personal Year. Some transformations might include a new commitment to a geographical location, relationship or career, freeing yourself from the confines of traumatic family history, or getting hired as a key player in a group project where you structure the project and support its implementation.

BENEFITS OF THE 4 PERSONAL YEAR

- You'll feel the positive results of following a step-by-step process.
- You'll feel empowered when you're working systematically with a practical project or an issue.
- You'll enjoy and have success when you pay attention to details.
- You'll have the opportunity to practice flexibility even as you're focused on completing a task.
- You'll feel stable and grounded.

CHALLENGES DURING THE 4 PERSONAL YEAR

- Be aware that if you struggle with the destructive aspects of the 4 Personal Year, you'll feel less than enthused about diving into all the hard work the year requires from you.
- Protect yourself from procrastination and stubbornness by embracing the fact that this isn't a year for fun and frolic; rather you're required to keep your nose to the grindstone and methodically set the foundation for what's to come.
- Be prepared to default into a "control freak" mode. Bypass the tendency to be bossy and instead focus on the good of a project as a whole, even if it's your marriage or relationship with your father/mother, rather than a work-related project.

During a matching 4 Life Path and 4 Personal Year, expect a year of intensity surrounding core issues related to:
- Developing and acting with stability and process.
- Developing flexibility, both physically and mentally.
- Fear of change and chaos.
- Non-commitment and irresponsibility.
- Responding to experiences confrontationally.

The 5 Personal Year

AFTER A YEAR OF WORK AND STUDY, this is a year that feels like you are living in ADHD time: it is a whirlwind and your energies are scattered. There are lots of ups and downs, so the key for this year is *flexibility*. Lots of unexpected opportunities are bound to come your way, so be open to trying new things. If you don't attempt to follow a strict plan you'll be better off. It's time to travel, not a time to make a long-term commitment.

People will find you wildly attractive during this year, so watch out. If single: Beware (but have fun). If committed: Warn and reassure your mate.

Take some downtime when you can. The key to surviving this year intact is to establish a light sense of routine and structure in your life despite the pull to do the opposite. That doesn't mean to restrict the flow of all the fun, adventurous energies coming your way. Quite the contrary. It does mean that in order to take full advantage of these electrifying energies and opportunities, you must operate with some sense of structure and discipline or else the chaos will take over and you won't reap the rewards this year offers you.

You'll be tempted to overindulge in behaviors that offer you a sense of escape: alcohol, drugs, sex, overwork, too much travel. Understand these are the tendencies you're working with and modulate yourself in order not to feel like the whole year is one big hangover.

PROJECT REDECORATE
Initiate small changes during the 5 Personal Year. This year supports your efforts in stepping off the beaten path and evaluating where you are in your life in terms of your relationship to living fearlessly and with verve. This year you can take a cooking class, distance yourself from relationships that are no longer serving you, or sky dive for the first time.

PROJECT REMODEL

Take concerted and persistent action as you come to terms with your tendency toward addictions during the 5 Personal Year. The energy surrounding you is all about escape and fast-moving fun. It can sweep you off your feet much like a passionate lover. Promise yourself you will have enough fun to remember it in the morning but not so much fun that yesterday is a blur.

PROJECT RENOVATE

Cultivate your sense of freedom during the 5 Personal Year. Some transformations might include a decision to separate or divorce your spouse, a decision to ditch your job without having another one lined up yet, or a decision to go for that sales job you've been offered that requires extra travel.

BENEFITS OF THE 5 PERSONAL YEAR

- You'll feel sensual and sexually attractive.
- You'll feel empowered when you're riding the wave of the energy of the year while also establishing healthy parameters around your actions.
- You'll have success when you embrace your magnetism and focus your intentions on something specific.
- You'll have the opportunity to move through boredom and into mastery of a subject or area of expertise.
- You'll feel free to choose what you want to do and when you want to do it.

CHALLENGES DURING THE 5 PERSONAL YEAR

- Be aware that even though this is a year of constant change, you may feel fear rather than fearlessness.
- Protect yourself from overindulgence and recklessness by embracing the fact you always feel better at the end of the day

when you have followed a plan, no matter how loosely structured.
- Be prepared to default into a teeter-totter mode: everything feels like it's going up and down, up and down. This is a great year to discern what freedom actually means to you and then begin steps to bring more of it into your life. In order for you to do this with success, you must be able to focus and follow through.

During a matching 5 Life Path and 5 Personal Year Number, expect a year of intensity surrounding core issues related to:
- Developing your definition of fearless, adventurous living.
- Developing a balance between over giving to others and self-centeredness.
- Understanding the ways that irrational fear stands in your way.
- Appreciating your vivaciousness and magnetism, and using those attributes in a healthy way.
- Responding to experiences without over dramatizing them.

The 6 Personal Year

AFTER THE CRAZINESS of the previous year, it's time to regroup, nurture, and be nurtured. You might feel a strong itch to redecorate, paint, or move; almost a feeling of "nesting." This year is also a prelude to the next year, because it holds the energies of evaluation and slowing down, if not externally, at least internally. You may be super busy on the outside, yet on the inside you are contemplative.

This is a year where your personal magnetism is at a peak. Big opportunities await you this year in both your career and your intimate life. It's a good year to get married or engaged if you have been hovering around that decision. It's also a year where you may seek a divorce, go through a breakup, or experience other relationship splits. This year is all about evaluating the relationships in your life.

You'll be offered challenges in balancing being generous and nurturing to others and to yourself in equal measure. You're required to step up and offer your unconditional love and support to those who are important in your life, yet you're also being called upon to allow yourself the same support. This might be a year where you're involved in supporting friends or family with a wedding, a graduation, the birth of a baby, a health crisis, or any activities that demand your nurturing presence.

PROJECT REDECORATE

Initiate small steps during the 6 Personal Year. This year supports your efforts in slowing down and evaluating your relationships. This is a great year to plan some small excursions with loved ones, give yourself some special attention in any way that feels good to you, or take on the responsibility for a new project you've wanted to do.

PROJECT REMODEL

Take concerted and persistent action to come to terms with a tendency to act self-righteous during the 6 Personal Year. The energy surrounding you is all about balancing the energies of nurturing, responsibility, and visionary projects. It can hold an intensity all its own, as you really dig deep into yourself to uncover what you do and don't want in your relationships. You might find yourself bowing out of friendships or commitments you have outgrown.

PROJECT RENOVATE

Cultivate your alignment with your inner desires during the 6 Personal Year. Some transformations might include a major breakup with a marriage or similarly committed relationship, commencement in working with the charitable organization you feel strongly about, or diving into a new project you've been thinking about for ages yet never had the courage to take seriously.

BENEFITS OF THE 6 PERSONAL YEAR

- You'll feel as though you are Yoda. Everyone wants your advice this year. Advise wisely and well, because people take what you say to heart.
- You'll feel empowered when you're finding ways to take care of yourself with the same focus and dedication that you care for others.
- You'll have success when you trust your ability to see the bigger picture while moving toward your goal in manageable steps.
- You'll have the opportunity to be supportive to your family and loved ones in different ways than you have in the past.
- You'll feel useful to others and grounded in your sense of yourself.

CHALLENGES DURING THE 6 PERSONAL YEAR

- Be aware that even though this is a year devoted to nurturing and responsibility, you might not feel all that excited about taking on this task.
- Protect yourself from a tendency toward perfectionism this year. You have too much going on; understand that good enough is good enough.
- Be prepared to feel as though the weight of the world rests on your shoulders. While this is a year for nurturing and paying attention to the loved ones in your life, make sure that you're part of the equation. You have to ask for what you need from others in order to get your own needs met.

During a matching 6 Life Path and 6 Personal Year, expect a year of intensity surrounding core issues pertaining to:

- Developing your ability to release your need to control your environment and the people around you.
- Developing compassion for yourself and others.
- Understanding that you're at your best when you're working for justice or a cause you feel strongly about.
- Appreciating the fact that you thrive in a domestic environment when you're balanced.
- Responding to people who seek your advice as a supportive, active listener, rather than responding to them with criticism and judgment.

The 7 Personal Year

THE ENERGY OF LAST YEAR was a perfect segue into the internal, contemplative energies of your 7 Personal Year. While you may still see yourself functioning fairly normally, this is a year where you'll be heavily involved in inner work. It's a spiritual year; meaning, you'll have many opportunities to test your sense of spirituality, however you define it. This is a year where your faith and trust could be tested. It's a time of deep contemplation or—if you're working with more destructive tendencies in this cycle—big feelings of being a victim in your life.

This is a time for introspection, meditation, and spiritual study. It's also a good time for counseling or therapy, energy work, and anything else that allows you deep personal growth.

You need to truly embrace *you* during this time. While the 2 Personal Year is all about "us," this is the "me" year in which the Universe is giving you full permission to contemplate your own navel. This may be a year where you are quiet and not as outwardly communicative as usual, so be clear when dealing with your relationships: Let your loved ones know it's not them you're responding to, it's just what you need this year.

You can almost become reclusive during this personal year and if you have a 7 Life Path Number, you feel this energy with amazing intensity. Often people report that difficult and painful events happen to them during a 7 Personal Year. It has the potential to rival the 9 Personal Year in terms of facing challenges like loss, letting go, health issues, or other events that people typically find hard to handle. It's a year to cultivate a balance between your intuition and your analytic mind.

PROJECT REDECORATE

Initiate small changes during the 7 Personal Year. This year supports your efforts to develop patience. This is a year to learn to meditate, join a hiking club, or finish writing your book.

PROJECT REMODEL

Make a concerted effort to come to terms with your tendency toward dwelling in the negative during the 7 Personal Year. Even though you feel as though you need to be needed, you'll struggle with the difficulties of opening yourself up to vulnerability. Some trial balloons might be to allow yourself to receive without feeling the overpowering impulse to give even more back, to allow yourself not to know the answer and be perfectly okay with not knowing, or to allow yourself to step away from giving unsolicited advice to people who really don't want to hear what you have to say.

PROJECT RENOVATE

It is time to take a look at your abandonment issues—big or small—during the 7 Personal Year. Some transformations might include coming to terms with your sense of spirituality—or lack thereof—checking yourself into rehab, or going on sabbatical to work on your research.

BENEFITS OF THE 7 PERSONAL YEAR

- You'll feel inspired to connect with your spirituality.
- You'll feel empowered when you connect the dots between mind, body, and spirit in a practical way that works for you.
- You'll have success when you embrace the internal journey the year brings you.
- You'll have the opportunity to see how dealing with your experiences with frustration does not serve you and is not necessary.
- You'll feel a deep need to delve into the ways that you can cultivate trust in yourself and in other people.

CHALLENGES DURING THE 7 PERSONAL YEAR

- Be aware that you may feel lonely this year.
- Protect yourself from feelings of isolation by scheduling some breaks for yourself: weekend trips, get-togethers with friends, or meet-ups with colleagues.
- Be prepared for defaulting into cynicism. This is a great year to discern what you really believe and how you want to act on that knowledge.

During a matching 7 Life Path and 7 Personal Year, expect a year of intensity surrounding core issues related to:

- Developing recognition of when you're being aloof out of self-protection.
- Developing a balance between your intuition and your thinking mind.
- Understanding the ways that your fear of making mistakes is

holding you back from pursuing your true purpose in life.
- Appreciating the way you can key into other people and just by a simple word or gesture make a huge difference in their lives.
- Responding to experiences without over dramatizing or being devastated when you (and other people) don't meet your high expectations.

The 8 Personal Year

THIS IS A YEAR TO FOCUS on money, finances, and personal power. During your 8 Personal Year, you can't help but wake up every morning, and going to sleep every night, thinking about your finances. This can be a year of financial abundance and of your financial life taking priority over other matters. You might be in work overdrive this year. Make sure to let your loved ones know you love them in every way you can so that they won't feel neglected.

On the other end of the spectrum, you might be working with the reality of the lack of abundance in your life, so while you're constantly thinking about money, you're thinking about all the money you don't have. While this is a good year for investing or simply reaping the financial rewards from foundations set in place during the previous years, if you haven't been diligent in working toward financial abundance, this is a year where financial losses might befall you.

You might feel under attack this year. You may feel that other people are not cooperating with you or supporting you in the way you'd like. You may even feel that you are undermining or sabotaging your own goals this year. The key is to balance your drive for financial success with care and heartfelt communication; then you'll be unstoppable.

It's a year where your sense of personal power will be tested. This is the time to retire from being a "doormat" for other people and to step up and embrace your personal power with integrity and from your heart. If money issues don't take center stage, issues relating to your personal power will be in the spotlight.

Caution: You might feel impulses toward greedy or shady dealings. Don't go for the easy money. Go for ethical, aboveboard behaviors in both your business and personal life.

PROJECT REDECORATE

This year supports your efforts in getting your finances in order by finally writing down a household budget, by investing money in whatever manner you feel is most advantageous to you, or by reevaluating your income and expenses and making decisions about how to begin to make more money.

PROJECT REMODEL

Make a concerted effort to come to terms with your tendency toward any feelings of powerlessness during the 8 Personal Year. This is a year to step up and engage with all of your personal power. If you are in an abusive relationship (either in your personal or business life), this is the year to say no to these relationships and regain control over your life.

PROJECT RENOVATE

It is time to think abundantly. Some transformations might include leaving a truly abusive relationship, cashing in on a big investment in order to start a new project, or come to terms with the ways you may be sabotaging yourself financially and come up with a game plan to change it.

BENEFITS OF THE 8 PERSONAL YEAR

- You'll feel powerful and dynamic.
- You'll feel empowered when you're in a position of "reaping what you have sown." This is a year of great rewards or huge disappointments, depending on the seeds you've planted in the previous years.
- You'll have success when you embrace the idea that money is a tool that can be used for the betterment of both yourself and for other people.
- You'll have the opportunity to use your intense power in whatever manner you choose; so choose wisely.
- You'll feel busy, directed, and ready to do whatever it takes to get things accomplished.

CHALLENGES DURING THE 8 PERSONAL YEAR

- Be aware that this can be a year of testing. You'll be tested in the realms of leadership, integrity, expansive thinking, and patience.
- Protect yourself from being a "bull-dozer" this year. You'll feel like you know what to do and how to get it done, yet you must also work with others and be open to the idea that other people might have good ideas that'll help you out.
- Be prepared for defaulting into your intimidation mode. It'll be easy to feel in a hurry and as though you are always on a deadline during the 8 Personal year. Understand that while you'll feel a fire underneath you, success will come more easily when you slow down enough to focus and respect other people in the process.

During a matching 8 Life Path and 8 Personal Year, expect a year of intensity surrounding core issues pertaining to:
- Developing your definition of abundance and acting on that vision.

- Developing time to step back and appreciate yourself and others in your life with a feeling of love and sweetness.
- Understanding that you might need encouragement to reach your capacity this year, so seek out your support team.
- Appreciating that sometimes your ego will get in your way. Get to know what that looks and feels like so that you can understand when it's happening, and bypass it when possible.
- Responding to your drive for wealth without defaulting to greed or money for its own sake.

The 9 Personal Year

THIS IS A YEAR OF COMPLETION, of unraveling, of letting go of the old to make space for change. This change will encompass possessions, relationships, job, geographical location, spirituality, health. All of it. It's all under review this year. And frankly, it might not be the most "feel good" year on record, yet if you know it's inevitable, why resist? If you take action to purge things from your life that aren't working out for you, and purposefully work to create constructive change during this time, this will offer positive momentum to the transitions that are taking place. You'll face obstacles, and yet you need to be absolutely persistent.

Life changes that are known to happen during a 9 Personal Year include: divorce, being fired from a job, the death of a close family member, having a baby, graduating from school, making a big geographical move, and coping with a serious health crisis. You'll survive. Not only will you survive, you'll go on to an even more expansive cycle in your life if you choose to let go and allow what is no longer serving you to fall away. All of these hard experiences are pushing you to grow and evolve. You can choose to give up or to use all of your difficulties as fuel to push you onward and upward into the next, higher realm of your life. It's totally up to you to choose defeat or empowerment. When we realize and come to a deep understanding that life is truly a series of painful, uncomfortable, joyful, invigorating, and profoundly moving events and experiences, then we can embrace all aspects of our experience: the good, the bad, and the ugly.

No one on the planet lives a life without pain or "unexpected" circumstances. If we can expect the unexpected and get over believing, "My life wasn't supposed to be like this," chances are we could all become more deeply engaged with working on the constructive aspects of what we truly came into the world to accomplish.

PROJECT REDECORATE

This year supports your efforts peeling away the layers and getting down to the core of who you really are and what you want in your life. This year you might consider beginning to write in a daily journal, learning to meditate, or taking a yoga class.

PROJECT REMODEL

Take concerted and persistent action to come to terms with your tendency looking back to the past with either an idyllic sense or with bitterness during the 9 Personal Year. The energy surrounding you is very powerful for anything having to do with completion, conclusions, or endings. You may find that you need to shift your job, move to another town, return to school, or any number of major transitions.

PROJECT RENOVATE

Cultivate the ultimate sense of *letting go* during the 9 Personal Year. Some transformations might include the death of loved one, a health crisis, a separation, or a divorce. You might find that a segment of your professional life comes to a close through retirement or other means. This may be a year that your last child moves out of the house or a year your first child is born.

BENEFITS OF THE 9 PERSONAL YEAR

- You'll feel a compulsion to reevaluate all aspects of your life and make decisions to become involved in some area of service with a humanitarian focus, big or small. You'll feel a great sense of compassion this year.
- You'll feel empowered when you know that this is a tumultuous year and so you need to meet up with all that comes your way with the least resistance.
- You'll have success when you have a solid spiritual base from which to operate, however you define your spirituality.
- You'll have the opportunity to redesign any aspect of your life that needs to be expanded or eliminated.
- You'll feel an undeniable intensity and urgency surrounding you and your decisions this year.

CHALLENGES DURING THE 9 PERSONAL YEAR

- Be aware that you'll be challenged with codependency issues and issues related to letting go of old attachments.
- Protect yourself from depression and anxiety by allowing this to be a year where you lay down the paddles and allow the Universe to guide your boat.
- Be prepared for defaulting into cynicism and intolerance, as you'll be challenged with needing to see the bigger picture even though that picture looks blurry at the moment.

During a matching 9 Life Path and 9 Personal Year, expect a year of intensity surrounding core issues of:

- Developing your ability to accept yourself and others just the way they are.
- Developing your ability to forgive both yourself and others for past injustices.
- Understanding the ways clinging to the old ways of doing things will bring about more pain than the actual pain involved in letting the old ways go.
- Appreciating your tenacity, resilience, and openhearted approach to life.
- Responding to obstacles as teachers rather than limitations.

Saturn Returns

ALONG WITH THE 1–9 Personal Year Cycle, there are two other important turning points you need to know about. Both are called "Saturn Returns." Career Intuitive Sue Frederick introduces the coupling of the Personal Year Cycle with Saturn Returns in her book *I See Your Dream Job* (St. Martin's Press, 2009). Frederick mixes the power of numerology with some key elements of astrology. Basically, there are two times in your life when the planet Saturn returns to where it was in your astrological chart when you were born. The first takes place when you're 28–29 years old. The second takes place when you're 58–59 years old. The importance of these powerful transitions shouldn't be underestimated, insofar as they'll have an overlapping effect on whatever you're experiencing during your regular Personal Year Cycle during those years.

These two transitions can be major turning points in your life. The energy that accompanies a Saturn Return is intense and powerful. These are points where you'll be forced to make

149

major, soul-searching decisions about the direction you're headed. If you choose to do "business as usual" after these transits, chances are good that you aren't going to be happy. Not at all. The vibration of a Saturn Return demands that you shake things up and make substantial changes. You'll experience such an intense need to take a different direction that the internal pressure to do so will be enormous despite how "crazy" heading in that new direction may seem.

Saturn Returns are times of major reevaluation: opportunities to redesign your current life, totally change course, or just keep a lid on it. Keeping a lid on it will always bring unwanted consequences, like health problems and depression. So I don't recommend that option. Whenever I feel depressed, I stop and ask myself: *What am I depressing? What am I holding down? What am I not allowing to surface in my life?* Those will be key questions for you also during both of your Saturn Return transitions.

It's interesting to listen to people in the media talk about their lives and indicate when they made huge, life-changing decisions. Take notice. You'll hear subjects of interviews over and over again say, "I don't know what happened, but when I was twenty-seven I just couldn't deal with it anymore," "When I was twenty-eight my whole world fell apart. That was when I made the decision to take a 180-degree turn in my life. I don't even know why" or "I finally started doing what I've always wanted to do" (and then you find out they were sixty when they started doing it). Perk up your ears and start listening when you hear people talking about when they experienced a major upheaval their lives. Oftentimes that upheaval coincided with their Saturn Return.

How Do I Use My Personal Year Cycles?

APPLYING THE KNOWLEDGE you glean from your Personal Year Number is a multifaceted process with many benefits. First, knowing that you are in a 9 Personal Year, for example, certainly can take some of the confusion and resistance out of a year of tumultuous transitions. It won't take the sting away; yet knowing that a year is meant to be a tough—or at least challenging—is worth the price of admission. That knowledge alone allows you to step back and view your life through a new lens and direct your focus on the tasks at hand.

Also make a note: Your Personal Year Cycles run from January 1–December 31, *not birthday to birthday*. Look again at how it is calculated and you'll see it is from the start of the year to the close of that same year. However, you'll experience *intensity* in the energies of the calendar year directly before and after your birthday.

When you fill out your worksheet outlining all of your Personal Year Cycles up until the present, you'll be able to excavate valuable information about yourself and your life. When you look back at your past Personal Year Cycles and locate the transition points from the 9 into the 1 Personal Years, try to remember what was happening in your life during those periods. This information can help you anticipate what may happen during your next similar transition.

Use this information to come up with a skeletal framework of what can be considered the "punctuation marks" in your life. You'll find that often when you're telling someone your life story, these are the moments that frame your story. For instance, my own Personal Year Cycle of endings and new beginnings looks like this:

- First 9–1 Personal Year transition (6–7 years old): *Moved to my favorite childhood home.*
- Second 9–1 Personal Year transition (15–16 years old): *Traumatic events at home.*
- Third 9–1 Personal Year transition (24–25 year old): *Had my first child.*
- First Saturn Return (29 years old/5 Personal Year): *Depressed, restless. Started graduate school.*
- Fourth 9–1 Personal Year transition (33–34 years old): *Mother's death. Graduated from graduate school.*
- Fifth 9–1 Personal Year transition (42–43 years old): *Got a divorce.*

My sixth 9–1 Personal Year transition is coming up soon. Because of my past transitions I know how to prepare for the changes, or at least I know there will inevitably *be* changes! Just knowing that gives me a leg up on making conscious choices during the upcoming transition.

Finally, knowing about your Personal Year Cycles can validate the ways you're feeling and help to support beneficial choices. For example, if I know I'm in a 4 Personal Year (a time for planting seeds and sharpening skill sets) and yet I feel the tendency to frolic and scatter my attention, I know that this won't be a satisfying or productive year for me. If I follow my impulses, instead of feeling good about all the partying I'm doing, I'll end up feeling lousy because I went against the energy and purpose of the year.

The bottom line is that when you are operating within the energies presented to you during your Personal Year Cycles, you'll have amazing support from the Universe to build your best life. Yet you must understand that change happens incrementally, in stages, on a foundation of building blocks constructed with conscious direction, intent, and focus. Just having an awareness of the "themes" to each of the nine Personal Years allows you to see all the components needed to redesign a life that pleases and fulfills the wildly optimal you.

THEMES TO REMEMBER

1 Personal Year: Building confidence and leadership, initiation, new beginnings, action

2 Personal Year: Slow and deliberate, "us" rather than "I," emotionally sensitive

3 Personal Year: Creative and fun, communicative, "getting out there"

4 Personal Year: Serious and hard-working, setting foundations, healing family wounds

5 Personal Year: Frenetic and fast-paced, filled with adventure, time for change

6 Personal Year: Nurturing of self and others, marriage and divorce, heightened responsibility

7 *Personal Year:* Contemplative and introspective, spiritual, learning

8 Personal Year: Money and personal power, active and hardworking, abundance/scarcity

9 Personal Year: Letting go and falling away, major transitions, loss, and resilience

First Saturn Return (28–29 years old): Major reevaluation period coupled with major shift in life.

Second Saturn Return (58–59 years old): Major reevaluation period coupled with major shift in life.

CHAPTER 4

YOUR LIFE STAGES AND CHALLENGES

THE FIRST TWO TOOLS helping you redesign your life are: 1) knowing your Life Path Number and 2) having a grasp on your Personal Year Cycles. The third and final tool we'll be working with is the tool of Life Stages and Challenges. In numerology, Life Stages are sometimes called "The Four Pyramids" or "Pinnacles." I choose to call them "Life Stages."

Calculating your four Life Stage Numbers, and the Challenges inherent within those Life Stages, is not so much a predictive tool—although it can be used to map out a clearer vision of your future—as a tool that offers support and guidance for your life decisions and actions. It can help you clarify your goals. Knowledge of your Life Stages is a platform upon which to construct your life in a more conscious and meaningful way.

The Formula for Calculating Your Life Stage Numbers

HERE'S HOW IT WORKS. Each Life Stage is a time of personal development. Together, the four Life Stages make up the blueprint of your entire life. Consider them like a master plan. Each Life Stage Number represents the energy that is emphasized during a period of several years. This is advantageous to know because if you're aware what energies are operating in your life with during each Life Stage, you can create more opportunities to achieve your goals, hopes, and dreams more fully and with less resistance.

Let me clarify that *your Life Path Number never changes*. If you are born with a 7 Life Path, you die with a 7 Life Path. Think of the Life Stage Numbers as the energy surrounding and influencing you during each defined period of your life in addition to your Life Path Number. The Life Stage energy sets the stage on which you— "the actor" —are performing.

Here is the basic formula for finding your four Life Stage Numbers. ***Digit down your birth date to three one-digit numbers (day, month, year). See the workbook for guidance.***

- First Life Stage = Month of Birth + Day of Birth
- Second Life Stage = Day of Birth + Year of Birth
- Third Life Stage = First Life Stage Number + Second Life Stage Number
- Fourth Life Stage = Month of Birth + Year of Birth

Formula to Calculate Your Age during Your Different Life Stages

NOW YOU MUST CALCULATE the age you are during your different life stages. Your age in every stage depends on the Life Path Number you identified back in chapter 2.

At this point, please go to FeliciaBender.com to get a downloadable copy of the *Redesign Your Life Workbook,* which contains worksheets for all of your numerological calculations like this one. Calculating your Life Stages and Challenges is slightly more complex than working with your Life Path and Personal Year numbers.

To calculate your age during your First Life Stage, take the number 36 and *subtract* your Life Path Number from it.

Example: If you are a 9 Life Path, subtract 9 from 36.
36 − 9 = 27

This means that your First Life Stage transpires from the *time of your birth until you're 27 years old.*

To calculate your age during your Second Life Stage, simply *add* 9 to the ending age of your First Life Stage.

Example: For the 9 Life Path, whose First Life Stage ended at age 27, we calculate:
27 + 9 = 36
Your Second Life Stage lasts from age 27 to age 36.

To calculate your age during your Third Life Stage, add 9 to the ending age of your Second Life Stage.

Example: For the 9 Life Path, whose Second Life Stage ended at age 36, we calculate:

36 + 9 = 45

Your Third Life Stage lasts from age 36 to age 45.

Your Fourth Life Stage starts at the end of your Third Life Stage. This age initiates the energy surrounding you for the rest of your life.

Example: For the 9 Life Path, whose Third Life Stage lasted until age 45, the Fourth Life Stage began at age 45.

Formula for Calculating Your Life Stage Challenge Numbers

KNOWING YOUR Life Stage Challenge Numbers and understanding their meaning can make all the difference to your happiness and success. To know what you're up against is often half the battle of being able to achieve your goals. Challenge Numbers are not meant to be *overcome*; rather they indicate what you must *become*. The issue here is that when a number presents itself to you as a challenge vibration, it is bombarding you with the *destructive* aspects of that number while *simultaneously demanding that you operate in the constructive aspects of the number.*

Here is how to calculate the Challenge Numbers for your Life Stages. Let me be clear: You must *subtract* numbers here rather than use addition. Another funny thing you need to know is that there are no negative numbers in numerology, so you actually can subtract a larger number from a smaller number. If you subtract a 9 from a 2, for instance, what you end up with is a 7. If you subtract a 7 from a 3, what you end up with is a 4.

See what I mean? It is like spinning the hands of a circular clock backwards around its face—except there are only nine "hours" instead of twelve. If it helps you to visualize it, go ahead and draw a circle and do your calculation manually.

Here is the basic formula for finding your Challenge Numbers.

- First Challenge Number = Day of Birth – Month of Birth
- Second Challenge Number = Year of Birth – Day of Birth
- Third Challenge Number = Second Challenge Number – First Challenge Number
- Fourth Challenge Number = Year of Birth – Month of Birth

In the next section, "The Life Stages and Challenges Reference Guide," I will take you through the meanings and definitions of the different Life Stage Numbers and Challenge Numbers so that you can get a better picture of your own life's master plan. This will be essential information for you as you set about doing your life redesign project.

Please don't skip over the entire trajectory of your Life Stages and Challenges to get to the stage you're in currently. I find that being able to reflect on the stages you've already gone through offers some surprising opportunities for emotional healing if you choose to use the information in that manner.

As I have investigated my own Life Stages and Challenges, I've challenged myself to get up close and personal about some of my emotional issues. For instance, when I calculated my Life Stages and Challenges and saw that I experienced an 11/2 First Life Stage, a lot of things came together for me. I was a very emotionally sensitive child, teen, and young adult. Looking back, there were many things that I can see I took entirely too personally and have hung on to those negative emotional experiences with a vengeance. Learning about my 11/2 First Life Stage energy has allowed me to forgive myself for certain things and also to forgive others for things they surely didn't even realize they'd done. Knowing the numerological Life Stage information has allowed me to look at my past through a wonderfully fresh lens.

It's been very freeing to backtrack and give myself new opportunities to heal issues from my past that perhaps were standing in my way to creating the wildly optimal me. So that has been worth the price of admission for me, so to speak. I hope you can find similar relief and transformation for yourself as you calculate your own Life Stages and identify the Challenges you faced in the past, are facing now, and will face in the future.

LIFE STAGES AND CHALLENGES REFERENCE GUIDE

NOW THAT YOU HAVE DETERMINED your four Life Stages and your Challenge Numbers for those stages, here are the basic characteristics that can guide you through, over, and around your particular Life Stage.

This reference guide is organized by Life Stage Number and Challenge Number. At the end of each segment there's a short list of the destructive aspects of each Challenge Number. Please keep in mind that this list is merely a glimpse of some of the *potential* extremes inherent to the Challenge Number. The Challenge Number by definition is confrontational; it challenges you to overcome the destructive energies while becoming the constructive energies associated with a particular Life Stage Number.

So for instance, if you show a 4 Challenge Number during one of your Life Stages, you might not feel as though you want to get up early and seize the day, work hard, set up lasting systems for yourself, work through old family wounds or concentrate on gaining as much knowledge as possible. You'll instead be challenged

160

with the flipside of the 4 energy and will more likely be compelled to sleep in late and go to bed late, feel lazy mentally, physically, and spiritually and refuse to see a bigger picture of your life. That's why it's called your "Challenge," because the negative energy entices you to stray from your more constructive purpose.

Knowing this, you could set up a system of accountability, monitor your tendency by journaling about it or maintaining a time log, commit to going to bed early, and hire a coach to point out your blind spots, for example. That's the advantage of knowing about a Challenge; it enables you to respond proactively to the energy that is influencing your behavior.

1 Life Stage

DURING THIS STAGE, you are focused on developing *independence, self-reliance,* and *individuality.* The primary energy during this phase of your life is to achieve mastery in these areas. This is a time spent developing your ability to express your individuality by cultivating original ideas, by leading and directing others, by attaining success and achievement in the material world, and by gaining recognition for those achievements.

STAGE ONE: Keep in mind that especially during a 1 Life Stage, all people and circumstances in your life are fully *on purpose;* these people and experiences are your teachers if you can perceive them in that light. When you have this number for a First Life Stage, chances are your youth is spent learning how to develop and use original ideas. You're called to lead and to rely on yourself without resorting to the downside of ego, stubbornness, and being self-centered or dominating. It's not necessarily a settling time because it's governed by exponential learning, which includes all the hard knocks that go with it.

STAGE TWO OR THREE: If you have a Number 1 for the Second Life Stage or Third Life Stage, you're being groomed for—and challenged with—embracing leadership and developing all that being an effective and inspirational leader entails. You're being called upon to focus intently on these aspects: courage, drive, vision, focus, determination, and, most of all, integrity. You might experience a certain degree of aggressiveness in your demeanor at this time. Your ability to get ahead is limited only by your own initiative during a 1 Life Stage.

STAGE FOUR: A Fourth Life Stage with a Number 1 is marked by what might be called imposing energy; meaning, any thought of slowing down or retiring is most likely not in the cards. Both challenges and changes will accompany this last stage of life and your accomplishments can be profound if you've mastered the art of leadership, direction, and expression of your own original ideas.

Warning: When you're being groomed by the Universe for a leadership position, you'll be required to be an intern first. This means that it's unlikely for you to magically be handed golden opportunities for success—and if you are, take them and run with them. Usually you'll have to construct your own opportunities through desire, focus, self-determination, and the ability to take a punch, get up, shake it off, and keep going.

1 Challenge

IF THE NUMBER 1 is a Challenge number in your blueprint, you are being called upon to *stand up for yourself, be true to yourself,* and *be self-reliant.* You're truly being called upon to step up to the plate and become a leader. This won't necessarily be a gift that simply falls into your lap; you will need to cultivate leadership qualities, trust in your vision, and hone your people skills so you can be most effective in getting the job done.

During this time, you're likely to feel dominated by others in one way or another—either professionally or in your relationships. This feeling of being dominated might lead you to be competitive and you might experience an overwhelming sense of needing to achieve above all else. Your challenge lies in your ability to recognize when you're being pulled into this negative vortex and instead focus your energies on controlling the ego and keep self-righteousness in check.

You're learning about self-reliance and how to solve your own problems—and perhaps the problems of others—independently. You need to cultivate your wit and intelligence and cast tendencies toward argumentation and resentfulness aside. Also cultivate your confidence. This is a period where you'll come under fire by critics and detractors. Don't allow the naysayers to stand in your way or deflate your vision.

Destructive Aspects of the 1 Challenge

FOR THE RECORD, these are some of the destructive tendencies that the 1 Challenge has the potential to bring into your experiences.

- Major or minor bouts with feelings of insecurity
- Becoming an aggressive "know-it-all"
- Getting caught up in "being right" at all costs
- Allowing addictions to overtake you
- Becoming extremely emotionally needy
- Feelings of ill health due to frustration

2 Life Stage

WHEN THIS IS YOUR Life Stage Number, you're being beckoned to envelop yourself in the elements of learning to *cooperate,
share, be considerate of others,* and *be at your best when you are in
harmonious relationships without sacrificing yourself in the process.*
That last item is the real obstacle.

Two is the number of partnerships, patience, balance, and
keeping fairness at the helm. Therefore this Life Stage is a time
where love takes front seat, whether it's through marriage or
partnership, parenting, or other experiences that have the elements of unconditional love at the core.

This is a time where you will be called upon to work on—and
perfect—your subtle art of relating. The 2 energy also has to do
with gathering and relating facts or data, perfecting details, and
being a team player whose strength lies in being of service in a
joyous and balanced way. Where precision and details are valued,
you'll be happiest with your contributions.

A 2 Life Stage immerses you in friendliness and harmony.
This energy asks you to pay attention to details and practice
patience and tact. It won't offer much recognition for all you do
during this time, so you must turn to yourself for acknowledg-
ment in order not to feel resentful.

STAGE ONE: If you experience a 2 First Life Stage, count on
being an overly-sensitive child who's easily hurt and who takes
on the emotions of those around you. Yet, since you're so young,
you won't realize you're feeling both your own emotions plus
those of everyone else. You may have difficulties with both verbal and emotional expression since you're overloaded with feelings that you're not yet mature enough to recognize and filter

out. Your mother is likely to be the strongest influence on you during the beginning of your lifespan.

STAGE TWO OR THREE: A Second Life Stage or Third Life Stage with a 2 influence will surround your life in the energies associated with working in balance with other people. This is a time that isn't so much "me" focused as "us" focused. When you master your ability to promote harmony in all things, show patience and a willingness to forgo credit based on your contributions to the whole, you'll be operating optimally. The work you engage in during this time is likely to be quite detailed and demanding. If you've been a content stay-at-home mom, for instance, it wouldn't be surprising to see this number in your Second or Third Life Stage.

STAGE FOUR: If you have 2 energy in your Fourth Life Stage, it's an opportunity to cultivate harmony. You can retire or continue to work, yet the key to feeling satisfaction and fulfillment will be patience, tact, and cooperation. Again, you'll need to control a tendency toward sensitivity. It doesn't serve you well to be at the mercy of overwrought emotions.

Warning: The 2 energy is super-duper sensitive. If you don't work with this energy mindfully your tendency will be to get your feelings hurt often and deeply. If you take every little thing personally, instead of cultivating your ability to relate well with yourself and others, you'll experience a substantial amount of pain during this time—not to mention a battering of your self-esteem in the process.

2 Challenge

THIS IS ONE of the most common Challenge Numbers because it revolves around *developing your sensitivity to all human relations* and *developing your sense of seeing other peoples' points of view.* This is a lifelong challenge for all of us, yet when it's your Challenge Number it'll present you with especially intense tests surrounding working with feelings of fear, not standing up for yourself, and lack of self confidence. The pain inherent in these lessons can be fierce. You'll be challenged with getting past basing your actions and decisions on what other people think or say about you. Again, the balance between giving to others constructively and giving to yourself in a way that isn't totally self-absorbed is part of this challenge period.

The challenge here is that you're being called to work with the energies of harmony, cooperation, and balance, and yet you are feeling none of this. Instead, you find it difficult to work with people because of your fear of criticism, or—*gasp!*—of being ignored. You feel huge doses of self-doubt, lack of self confidence, and there's always that nagging worry (sometimes tipping into paranoia) that other people are judging you.

So you can see that the challenge is to understand the destructive aspects of the sensitivity of the 2 energy so that you can strive toward incorporating the constructive aspect instead. This would include using your keen sensitivities as a strength because you're so attuned to others and what they're feeling. If you're wearing your "psychic armor," you can use that to your advantage with all of your interactions.

During this period you're faced with great difficulties in asserting yourself and making solid decisions. You might shy away from positions of responsibility and authority because you're so emotionally tender. This can be a great time to accumulate wisdom as you're offered the opportunity time and time again to show patience and pay close attention to detail in all you do.

Your mantra for the 2 Challenge: Don't take anything personally. This is a time for slower, more deliberate growth, rather than seeking quick or immediate gain or results. Respect this more "quiet" stage in your life. Frustration only leads to more frustration.

Destructive Aspects of the 2 Challenge

FOR THE RECORD, these are some of the destructive tendencies that the 2 Challenge has the potential to bring into your experiences.

- Becoming defensive, self-absorbed, and angry to the point of being irrational
- Stubbornness and taking unfair actions
- Feeling unworthy to the point of allowing abuse
- Feeling resentful and unacknowledged for things you do for others
- Unable to follow through on things you want to do (for example, finish school, train for a job)
- Health issues, particularly in the joints

3 Life Stage

WHEN A 3 LIFE STAGE comes, get ready to *dig into your emotions* and *express yourself.* This is a time to get to know your inner life intimately, to identify and deal with your emotions, and to cultivate your creativity in all its forms. This is a time when you'll have no other choice except to dig deep to locate your underlying emotions and learn to communicate these with clarity and purpose. If you attempt to hold your feelings and ideas in, you'll implode. Now is the time to allow yourself and others to see the true creative and emotional you.

Honestly, this Life Stage is set up for light, enjoyable activities that support joy and expression. This energy is supportive of travel, social activities, friendships, and entertainment. You may feel affectionate and certainly you feel the push to be outgoing during a 3 Life Stage. The foundation is being poured for growth and development of personal expression, particularly verbal expression. Even if you haven't felt particularly "artistic" or "creative" before, now you are likely to feel drawn toward participation in artistic creation of one kind or another.

The 3 vibration is aligned with the joy of the present moment. Long-term plans made during this stage might not come to fruition exactly the way you planned them. It's all about being with people, having some fun, and acting with a youthful attitude. It can be an "easy come, easy go" stage, where variety and movement trump hunkering down and making things happen. Think. Dream. Imagine. Create. These are your key components for the 3 Life Stage.

STAGE ONE: While it sounds rather breezy, if the number 3 shows up during your First Life Stage, it offers many challenges. While there may be lots of opportunities to develop and pursue artistic and creative potentials, chances are you won't recognize them or be willing to work at making them come to fruition this early in life because you lack the wisdom and experience that comes with age. So instead, there's a tendency to scatter your energies or perhaps to work on fleeting ideas. Better yet: You may just be having too much fun to worry about the future. The best spin: The 3 First Life Stage will encourage the development of a creative career.

STAGE TWO OR THREE: If you're in your Second or Third Life Stage, the 3 energy pertains to good friends and happy relationships, joy, gratitude, the pleasures of life, and creative self-expression. This is a time where your responsibilities and accomplishments are greatly dependent on your social demeanor and communication skills. You may be presented with opportunities to write, speak, design, or take a job in the entertainment industry. This time is marked by imagination and feelings.

Great news: If you're nurturing this number's healthy aspects during your Life Stage, it has a natural attraction for money and an easier life full of creativity where you're drawn to encourage and inspire others. You could even become interested in some aspect of the healing arts.

STAGE FOUR: If a Number 3 shows up for your Fourth Life Stage, there's a good possibility for travel and social activity. Often this is accompanied with a freedom from financial worry. It can be a very comfortable final stage in your life that is supportive of all your creative endeavors.

Warning: You'll feel that with the 3 energy, you can get easily scattered, distracted, and drained. The 3 energy is so curious, you'll want to learn something and then quickly move on to the next thing. You would benefit from developing more groundedness and a sense of self-discipline in order to take full advantage of this joyful and happy number.

3 Challenge

IF YOU HAVE A 3 CHALLENGE, you're learning to identify your feelings and to speak from your heart. It's a time where you're truly learning and mastering one of the major teachings of the 3 vibration: Your words have a profound impact on your life.

Sometimes the challenge resides in taking yourself and your feelings seriously; it may feel easier to use humor or criticism to mask your feelings. Or perhaps your challenge will be in taking yourself *too* seriously.

Some of the tendencies that the 3 vibration brings with it are the propensities for superficiality, exaggeration, self-centeredness, moodiness, and scattered energy. What this Challenge Number is inviting you to do is to use your creative energy to develop your positive, happy, loving, and inspirational spirit. Wasting 3 energy is like throwing away a priceless gift. It's the vibration of pure happiness. What more could a person ask for in life than that?

You might feel the compulsion to do too many things at once during a Life Stage that has a 3 Challenge. Despite your heightened imagination and gift for words—both written and verbal—this challenge will knock you over with a "block" when you want to express yourself effectively and honestly.

Even though you know you should be "out there" cultivating friends and business associates, you'll feel the urge to bury your head in the sand and a general malaise you can't seem to shake—or at least not for long. Instead of experiencing the great joyous vibrations the 3 has to offer, you'll instead be bombarded with joy's opposite. You'll struggle with feelings of negativity even to the point of becoming defensive and reclusive.

You may have a talent or desire to practice your talents for writing, acting, or speaking, yet you're reluctant to involve yourself with these activities because the thought of facing criticism is overwhelming. So you turn to expressing yourself with a negative emphasis as cynicism or ruthless judgment, or you might hide your creative talents behind a façade of withdrawal and feelings of shyness. You're being called to develop yourself in a social and creative way. You must jump over the destructive landmines along your path.

Destructive Aspects of the 3 Challenge

FOR THE RECORD, these are some of the destructive tendencies that the 3 Challenge has the potential to bring into your experiences.

- Experiencing such a sense of self-doubt that you don't move forward in your life
- Becoming an emotional sponge and experiencing severe emotional sensitivity
- Acting out of criticism and judgment
- Dwelling in negativity
- Shutting down, withdrawing, and becoming emotionally unavailable
- Attempting to get what you want through manipulation rather than stating it clearly
- Developing physical illness (especially in the intestinal tract) and depression

4 Life Stage

A 4 LIFE STAGE is the period of your life where you're being called to build your life with solid, stable foundations that'll last. This is often a period of time where you're drawn toward purchasing—or actually building—a home and concentrating your efforts on career and family.

This isn't a particularly light-hearted and fun time because you're learning and being tested by issues related to *organizing, setting up good systems, patience, hard work, endurance, working step by step,* and *moving ahead methodically.* This stage is for designing and pouring the proper foundation for your future life. It's a practical time where you're putting your ideas into the material world and manifesting your vision with discipline, limitations, and a serious attitude. Frankly, it's not a time to mess around. There's not a lot goofing off during this period.

You're being immersed in the energies that support a practical and realistic approach to life. So a demand for order, system building, and organization is key. The 4 Life Stage encourages you to be dependable, conscientious, and reliable. Determined and somewhat relentless effort is required and you may feel a strong compulsion and emotional need to immerse yourself in work during this Life Stage. When you do, you'll thrive on that energy.

STAGE ONE: Experiencing a 4 First Life Stage sets you up for a demanding childhood and adolescence. You might find your economic circumstances demand more concerted effort and hard work. This can also be a stage of life devoted to the pursuit of your education. In either event, it's unlikely you'll be involved in the normal frivolity of life because of the intensity of your schedule.

STAGE TWO OR THREE: A Second Life Stage or Third Life Stage with a 4 emphasis will fuel your ability to get ahead in the world and achieve—not so much because of innate talent as much as your drive and ability to out-work the competition. You might find some economic limitations during this Life Stage, set in your path to test your commitment to building solid and steady foundations while not being beaten down by obstacles and limitations.

STAGE FOUR: A Fourth Life Stage imbued with the 4 energy will most likely not allow you to slow down or retire in the way you might desire or expect. Four isn't a leisurely vibration, so it doesn't even recognize the notion of "retire" or "slow down." The important factor here is to do the work and feel good about the sense of accomplishment. There is a possibility that economic conditions will control your ability to slow down or retire.

The 4 Life Stage teaches you that your effort is what counts. The upside: If you take this energy seriously and build a strong foundation, you'll reap the benefits for the rest of your life.

Warning: The 4 energy offers with it a bevy of teachers. As you're challenged to build something of lasting value, you're setting up your future relationship with money, your ability to meet deadlines, your ability to institute effective systems, and your way of dealing with limitations.

4 Challenge

WHEN YOU'RE MET with a Number 4 Challenge, you are *meant to learn about the value of discipline, organization, practicality, hard work,* and *thrift*. Take this to heart: This isn't an easy challenge. It's full of restrictions and limitations that are demanding you learn how to succeed and work within these boundaries.

It's also a time where you're challenged with learning to set your own personal boundaries with others, learning to temper impatience, stubbornness, narrow-mindedness, and self-righteousness. With the 4 Challenge, you are being pulled to slow down, create a clear plan with obtainable goals, and then work tirelessly to achieve them.

The 4 Challenge also suggests a difficulty with work. Either you are challenged with not wanting to work at all, not liking the work you are "forced" to do, or problems completing tasks and working with efficiency. You may also exhibit tendencies to be careless and lack a sense of practicality. With this number, it's difficult not only to focus on work and obligations, but equally as difficult even to see what the real issues surrounding work and obligations are. You might not feel that you're being lazy. You might feel you're just unlucky. Or make excuses about it. You get the idea.

With a 4 Challenge, it's vital to learn patience, understanding, and the practical and effective way to deal with what you might consider mundane responsibilities. You'll most likely also be challenged to learn the importance of working within the parameters of a time schedule, showing up on time and when you say you will, and managing your downtime constructively.

Destructive Aspects of the 4 Challenge

FOR THE RECORD, these are some of the destructive tendencies that the 4 Challenge has the potential to bring into your experiences.

- Feelings of discouragement and confusion, often resulting in you feeling like a victim
- Being undependable, uncommitted, lazy, and irresponsible
- Making the same mistakes over and over again
- Allowing your relationships within your family to influence decisions negatively
- Avoidance of, and difficulties with, systems and processes
- Being prone to panic attacks when feeling overwhelmed

5 Life Stage

WHEN YOU HAVE a 5 Life Stage, get ready for what I call an "ADHD experience." This is a time for *change* and *uncertainty*. It feels as though you're experiencing life without a filter. In this Life Stage, vivacious, unbridled energy surrounds you and it's hard to know what direction to go or what to grasp onto. Ultimately, this is a time for loosening up patterns of restriction you have held on to in the past. The 5 Life Stage is all about developing a new sense of *freedom, liberation,* and *adventure.*

Change is the mantra for this period of your life—and that means change in *everything* from career direction and business decisions, to spirituality and health, marriage and divorce. You name it. It's all up for review during this highly energized portion of your life. If you're forward thinking and ready for a shakeup, this can be an brilliant time of transformation—but not without the pain associated with growth. This is *not* a time to nest or settle down; instead you'll find yourself being drawn into the public world.

The major focus of a 5 Life Stage is to learn to be adaptable and flexible. Remember: What you resist will persist. Don't resist this cataclysmic energy, yet also avoid impulsive decisions, including the strong urge to run away and avoid whatever you're experiencing. This too shall pass.

STAGE ONE: A 5 First Life Stage can be a difficult period because it's hard to find the stability to establish yourself, develop a sense of who you are, and set the foundations for what you want in adult life. Perhaps you end up moving quite often during this First Life Stage and it requires that you change schools and friends often. The 5 energy invites you to live by your own rules in many ways during this early time, which can be great for you, if well-managed. Most likely you'll find yourself getting into trouble. You're likely to experience a good amount of impulsiveness and a craving for unbridled independence during this early stage.

STAGE TWO OR THREE: If in the Second Life Stage or Third Life Stage, the vibration of the 5 supports your ability to progress and achieve in a fast-moving, highly fluctuating environment.

Adaptability is critical to your healthy progress during this stage. Your desire for—and sense of—freedom is quite powerful and significant during this Life Stage. You must be careful not to get too carried away and damage relationships or partnerships because of your unyielding urge for freedom, travel, and adventure.

STAGE FOUR: The 5 energy that guides your Fourth Life Stage results in a continuously fast-paced life. This won't be your road to a laconic retirement. Change and variety continue to present themselves and this can be an interesting stage of your life. In many cases, the 5 energy at the final stage of life brings with it freedom from overarching financial or domestic worries.

Warning: Because the 5 Life Stage is a time to expect the unexpected (and change is usually difficult for all of us) this period in your life can be exciting and yet unsettling. It'll often prove to be a transformational time accented with restlessness, activity, and a distinct desire to get outside of your own box. There also may be the tendencies to quit something before it's completed, to be promiscuous in your sexual life, or to habitually overindulge in food, drugs, alcohol, or gambling. Balance is key and a huge test during this 5 Life Stage.

5 Challenge

THE CHALLENGE INHERENT in the 5 is that you'll feel a little crazy. This energy is highly charged and quite intense. Most likely you'll feel like you've been hit over the head with a hammer. Think about how you've felt during the 5 Personal Years you've already lived through in your Personal Year Cycle: That's just a small glimpse of the feelings surrounding this longer segment of your life. Impatience, restlessness, and a relentless desire for personal freedom are at the core of your challenge. This is *the* time to mindfully become free from limiting behaviors. The problem with that is that under this challenge, being mindful is particularly hard.

With this challenge, you'll find yourself being extremely impulsive and unstable. You'll want to try everything at least once, so there's a chaotic and uncontrollable aspect to this vibration. Change will be inevitable, yet it must be handled in a thoughtful, meaningful, and controlled manner. You'll be pulled toward evading responsibility rather than committing to healthy and constructive change. All in all, this challenge requires that you learn, as early on as possible, to reign in your reckless tendencies and to monitor your impulses. Getting caught up in your trauma-drama will never serve your higher purpose.

Destructive Aspects of the 5 Challenge

FOR THE RECORD, these are some of the destructive tendencies that the 5 Challenge has the potential to bring into your experiences.

- Feelings of chaos resulting in either emotional paralysis or bad judgment
- Living a life of pure self-indulgence and lack of discipline
- Being irresponsible and unfocused
- Becoming fully immersed in addiction to food, sex, alcohol, drugs, or overwork
- Living with a victim mentality and flitting from relationship to relationship, job to job
- Health issues, including mental health, adrenal system burnout, injuries, and accidents

6 Life Stage

LOVE, DUTY, RESPONSIBILITY, and *family* are the hallmarks of any 6 Life Stage. This is a stage in your life that is immersed in the energies of nurturing. You may choose to nurture your career or your family—or even your pets or employees—yet you can't avoid these years that are devoted to nurturing those around you, embracing your sense of responsibility, and balancing giving to others and giving to yourself simultaneously.

If your giving is lopsided and you give, give, give to everyone else and leave nothing for yourself, you'll certainly experience the difficult lessons that accompany that imbalance. Or if your behavior is lopsided in the opposite direction, where you're self-involved and self-absorbed at the expense of giving freely to others, you'll certainly experience the difficult lessons that accompany that imbalance. You must achieve balance within yourself and your chosen family.

This is the stage where you'll feel the irresistible urge to establish or intensify your involvement with home, children, and the beautification of your surroundings. The 6 energy also carries with it a vibration associated with a commitment to community and humanitarian service of some kind, and so this might be a period of time that you'll feel compelled to be involved in some aspects of these services.

You can make considerable money during this Life Stage when you are solidly focused on your visionary contributions and service. This is also most certainly the "love and marriage" stage with intense focus on babies and the home. It can also be the "marriage and divorce" stage when the marriage as it stands can no longer be sustained.

One of the major influences of this 6 Life Stage is experiencing such an overwhelming sense of responsibility that brings with it an undeniable feeling of restriction and being tied down. The bottom-line is that you're learning about responsibility and nurturing, plain and simple. You'll learn what's required and when enough is enough by setting your boundaries. It's a time where you're developing knowledge of what's really in your heart and acting on it with compassion.

STAGE ONE: As a younger person in the midst of a 6 Life Stage, you're likely to find yourself knee-deep in duty and responsibility related to home and family. This may be because of the pressures you experience in your family with parents and siblings, or you may find yourself entering into premature marriage at an early age. Often this energy causes you to experience controlling circumstances from a parent or another authority figure.

STAGE TWO OR THREE: If you have the 6 vibration in your Second life Stage or Third Life Stage, you might find great achievement through accepting increasing levels of responsibility and interacting with diplomacy in whatever you do during this period. Home and family often take precedence over business, or at least meld with it. It's a time for you to attend primarily to the demands of family and friends rather than to the development of yourself as an individual.

STAGE FOUR: If you have a 6 Fourth Life Stage, the vibration brings with it the rewards and pleasures of family, friends, and security. You'll most likely act on your feelings of philanthropy. This is a stage where *giving back* is vital to your innate sense of well-being and purpose in the world.

Warning: The 6 vibration is such a high-frequency vibration that it tends to idealize the world, people, relationships, and even the self. This results in stubbornness and being overly opinionated. Attempt to temper those tendencies before they cause an imbalance in your life.

6 Challenge

WHEN YOU EXPERIENCE a 6 Challenge during one of your Life Stages, you'll most likely feel burdened or overwhelmed by family obligations. You're learning to serve others and strike a balance between honoring your commitments to them with your commitments to yourself. This is no small task. Remember: Even if you're able to achieve some semblance of balance of giving to yourself during this time devoted to nurturing others and learning about responsibility, you can't and shouldn't try to avoid caring for others under the influence of a 6 Challenge. If you're operating with the destructive tendencies of the 6 Challenge, you may be myopically self-centered rather than generous and giving.

This Challenge is often related to the energy of codependency, enmeshment, and giving for misguided reasons. Rest assured that you'll be alerted when you're taking care of others in an unhealthy way during this 6 Challenge.

You're prone to demanding extraordinarily high standards from other people and of yourself, which is in itself a setup for frustration and unhappiness. There's no way others could live up to your expectations. If leaning toward the challenges of the 6 vibration, you're apt to come across as authoritarian, intolerant, and self-righteous. If you don't step back into the constructive aspects of the 6 energy, your tendency during this time may well be to get lodged in cynicism, criticism, and judgment.

Avoiding friction in relationships by emphasizing harmony, using diplomacy at every turn, and allowing others to set their own paces and live their own perfectly imperfect lives will be the key strategies for rising above the challenges of the 6 vibration. Ultimately, your challenge lies in learning, embracing, and practicing unconditional love and acceptance.

Destructive Aspects of the 6 Challenge

FOR THE RECORD, these are some of the destructive tendencies that the 6 Challenge has the potential to bring into your experiences.

- Feelings of superiority and thoughts of judgment
- Being angry and disappointed with others and yourself to the point of cynicism
- Becoming self-absorbed and uninterested in helping or supporting others
- Becoming such a perfectionist that you feel paralyzed and fearful
- Living in denial of your emotional life
- Health issues that are often chest related (including asthma)

7 Life Stage

INTROSPECTION AND STUDY are the key ingredients of the 7 Life Stage. This is a segment of your life where you're beckoned to *explore your inner world through study, research, intense introspection,* and *soul development* in whatever manner you choose to pursue it. You'll experience wanting to be reclusive, as your focus turns mainly toward advancing your experience and knowledge in your area of specialization. This is a time mixed with analysis, gaining knowledge, and huge leaps in your intuitive capabilities.

By taking the time to develop spiritually under the influence of this 7 energy, you're setting yourself up for gaining substantial wisdom and skill, setting yourself apart from others in your ability to explain the unexplainable, and using your gifts to encourage others to seek and find their own truth and wisdom. As you find yours, you'll then be prepared to assist others find theirs.

Intrinsic to this vibration is a strict focus on learning, investigating, and gaining skills. You'll be pulled inward during the 7 Life Stage, so chances are high that you'll become a bit of a loner during this time—as opposed to during other stages in your life when you'll feel more open and outgoing. Your comfort zone will reside most distinctly in working alone or at least with few restraints.

While marriage is not out of the question, it'll take concerted effort for both partners to make it work during your 7 life stage. You might even find yourself uninterested or unconcerned with material matters and shy away from involvement in practical affairs. This could result in limited finances or even physical disabilities.

STAGE ONE: If you experience a 7 First Life Stage, it can be difficult because it means you will probably struggle with feeling alone and like you don't belong. Expect dramatic life experiences during this time that serve as teaching tools for your journey. It's a time when you're a serious student and—whether or not you can identify it as such—when you're motivated by inner yearnings. A First Life Stage accompanied by the 7 vibration can be a difficult and confusing time.

STAGE TWO OR THREE: If you experience this vibration in your Second or Third Life Stage, you'll be offered an opportunity to refine and specialize your skills down to a fine art if you so choose. Unless you're directly involved with some sort of research, religious, or philosophical endeavors, progress during this Life Stage can feel painfully slow. The benefits to your 7 Life Stage won't be seen in your material or financial realm as much as in your spiritual life and internal realm.

STAGE FOUR: As a 7 Fourth Life Stage, your spiritual development will be undeniable. You'll be called upon to teach others what you've learned. Continued time for study, development, contemplation, and higher learning are keys to this final Life Stage. The 7 vibration at this point in life requires detachment from the practical realms and putting a renewed focus on more philosophical thinking and relating. You may find it difficult to relate to people during this time, so it's best to seek out like-minded souls with whom to share ideas. Be patient and open though. People will come to you to hear what you have to say because of the wisdom and knowledge you have cultivated and gained through your life experiences. It's part of this Life Stage to become a master teacher and share your wisdom with others.

Warning: Does this Life Path sound as if it called you be a reclusive monk or the equal of Mother Teresa? Not so! Despite the concentration on your internal journey, you still need to live in the physical world and you'll happily go out and dance the night away at a party, enjoy passionate lovemaking with your sweetheart, and hold down a job. You can do those things, but this vibration also strongly requires you to allow yourself the time, energy, and space needed to focus and study all realms of experience.

7 Challenge

THE 7 COMPETES with the 4 energy in terms of the seriousness associated with its vibration. While the 7 demands inner exploration, the chances of feeling alone and isolated are common. Contemplating the intricacies of life and spirituality isn't mastered in a weekend seminar. Nor is it mastered in a lifetime. Yet that's the task you're being called to focus upon. Often there is a big "test" or some serious repression or avoidance during a Life Stage that has a 7 Challenge.

Remember: The key lesson for a 7 Challenge is to understand that all your experiences—especially those that occur during this particular Life Stage—are fuel for your growth. *Develop trust in yourself.* All that you experience during this period of life is meant to hone your powers of analysis and observation, intuition, and spirituality. You'll be asked to trust your analytic mind *and* your highly developed intuition.

During a period with a 7 Challenge you'll be faced with difficulties brought on by your discomfort with your own inner thoughts and feelings. This could feel like detachment from people and situations or like tumultuous unexpressed and unresolved emotions. You might feel exasperated and helpless, as though you're a hapless victim of life who is unable to change or improve his or her situation or circumstances. There's also a strong tendency to chronically complain and criticize while offering no solutions to your perceived problems.

More challenging aspects of the 7 vibration might lead you to express everything you say or write in a negative manner. You may feel the impulse to avoid your feelings by putting up a wall of pride and aloofness. This is your opportunity to develop faith in your own abilities rather than to rely on the opinions of others or dwell on your limitations.

Destructive Aspects of the 7 Challenge

FOR THE RECORD, these are some of the destructive tendencies that the 7 Challenge has the potential to bring into your experiences.

- Withdrawing through drugs, alcohol, sex, or spending your life online
- Either isolating yourself totally from the world or being unable to spend any time alone
- Avoiding work by being scattered, unfocused, and overly emotional
- Avoiding your own life by immersing yourself in someone else's (for example, the life of a family member, business partner, or friend)
- Becoming overly focused on money and material objects
- Health-related issues like addiction and depression

8 Life Stage

MONEY, BUSINESS, AUTHORITY, ethics, personal power, and abundance: These are the key elements in any 8 Life Stage. This is the stage where you're bombarded with opportunities to embrace and define your personal relationship with *power, money,* and *achievement*. It has an intense focus on matters of responsibility, efficiency, power, authority, leadership, and management of financial affairs.

Sounds exciting, right? Yet under the influence of the 8 Life Stage vibration your judgment will be tested over and over again and your career usually becomes your top priority. This isn't a particularly easy walk in the park. Chances are this Life Stage will require you to make some substantial shifts in your life and your relationships. While your opportunities for achievement, recognition, and financial success are heightened, it'll require a lot of strength, courage, and tenacity to do so. This isn't an easy Life Stage; it'll demand a lot from you and won't let up.

The 8 Life Stage is also tricky because, while its vibration supports all things relating to money, power, and authority, its vibration is unyielding in its demands that you get there through the use of the utmost ethics, honesty, integrity, solid leadership, and feelings of abundance—not just feelings of wanting to be "rich" or "wealthy." The highest form of the 8 vibration has to do with giving as you're receiving, with no strings attached, and from the clarity of your heart.

Aspects of the 8 Life Stage are: status, success, recognition, business, and commercial activity. If you keep with it, this Life Stage is set up to usher in improvements in your financial and personal power realms. The focus is on creative practicality with an emphasis on organizational and management skills and abilities. Emotions are downplayed and business acumen is at a peak.

STAGE ONE: If yours is an 8 First Life Stage, chances are that you may become involved and interested in business or commercial activity at a very young age. You may be the kid who mows lawns and starts his own business or perhaps you tap into a more aggressive 8 energy and find another money-making endeavor that surprises the adults around you. Your focus and dedication to your entrepreneurial enterprise is unyielding. Yet you most likely will face limitations and restrictions, which you'll find these frustrating or just downright debilitating. You excel at practical thinking.

STAGE TWO OR THREE: If you encounter an 8 vibration during your Second or Third Life Stage, you're apt to find yourself in the executive world—or you could be married to an executive. You're required to rely more on rational judgments and less on emotional impulses. You're single-mindedly focused on your ambition and achievement of great financial success, power, and authority.

STAGE FOUR: With a Fourth Life Stage, you're not geared toward quiet retirement. The development and culmination of status, wealth, and power can define this period—given that you act on both business principles and spiritual principles. This is your time to give back in substantial ways by using your gifts of money, power, and influence to help others. Thinking with the power of abundance and of giving back will support you in establishing a great and lasting legacy.

8 Challenge

WHEN THE 8 IS YOUR Challenge Number, you're being called upon to think big, step up to the plate, and get it done. Achievement is expected during this period and so, of course, this will also be your obstacle. People who experience an 8 Challenge either make it or break it—much in the same way that this happens with the 8 Life Path. It's a difficult Challenge, yet if you realize that you're supposed to be making money, supposed to be successful, perhaps you can shift out of the negative experiences and thoughts surrounding money and abundance and understand that this Life Stage could be the time of your life in which you experience your greatest financial success. When you're in your groove, you're in the peak of both your financial and your spiritual abundance, because you'll be giving most generously.

Your destructive pull will be toward greed, and you'll believe that satisfaction can only be gained by accumulation and safeguarding. You might experience great difficulty and effort in your attempts to gain money status and power, often to the exclusion of all else. Family life and relationships suffer during this challenge since all your focus is on yourself and on your financial achievement (or lack thereof). You're being called to use your ability to earn money and acquire status and power with a sense of balance and with a strict sense of ethics and philanthropy.

Warning: The caution here is to engage in all you do with your authentic self, with ethics and honesty and without greed and malice. If you lean toward the more destructive aspects of the 8 energy, there will be a price to pay. *The 8 Challenge also signals that you need to stop giving away your power.* This is a period of development where you're being groomed to fully embrace your sense of personal empowerment and learn to empower others.

Destructive Aspects of the 8 Challenge

FOR THE RECORD, these are some of the destructive tendencies that the 8 Challenge has the potential to bring into your experiences.

- Suppressing your power by choosing poverty, homelessness, or other ways to avoid achievement in your life
- By not focusing on your own relationship with money and instead focusing on everyone else's through jealousy, bad mouthing, and indulging in feelings of disgust
- Focusing only on material gain at the expense of everything else
- Being arrogant, unyielding, and uncompassionate
- Becoming lazy and feeling bored with life
- Health-related issues like addiction and mental illness

9 Life Stage

IF YOU HAVE A 9 LIFE STAGE, you're expected to show the world what a true humanitarian looks and acts like on a day-to-day basis. You're developing the attributes of *compassion, love, ethics,* and *tolerance*—combined with a big dose of inspiring and uplifting others through your wisdom and love. If this sounds like a big order to fill, *it is.* The 9 Life Stage is marked by emotional crises because you're being asked to end and let go of all matters in your life that no longer serve you and your higher purpose. No matter how scared you are—and it will bring up a reservoir of fear—this is a time for gaining wise maturity and healing your emotional issues.

Because of the intensity of this vibration and the over-arching perseverance and wisdom it requires, this isn't considered an easy Life Stage. It's a segment of life that demands the ultimate releasing of all that has held you back, of all of the painful stories you have continued to tell yourself about your past—particularly those that relate to your family relationships. The ultimate healing can take place during this Life Stage if you invite it in.

Remember: While this may be a Life Stage that appears to be thankless and filled with obstacles, it isn't true. There's plenty of potential for anything you want during this time when you're fully committed to playing your role in letting go. When you surrender, all good things come to you. *This is a time where you can literally create your own reality.* Money, good fortune, loving relationships, vibrant health, purposeful living: These are all possible during a 9 Life Stage.

STAGE ONE: With a 9 Life Stage at the beginning of your life, the influence of its vibration may be barely noticeable. Selflessness is an attribute that's developed over time and young children must first learn their identity for themselves before doing selfless service in a healthy and productive manner. Yet when you experience a 9 First Life Stage, you may be a child who is the friend to the "underdog," who's a protector of the kids who get bullied, those who are handicapped, or those who are ostracized in some way by other kids. You may be a bit of an outsider yourself as you attend to those on the fringes.

STAGE TWO OR THREE: A Second or Third Life Stage directed by the 9 vibration might set the stage for expression of emotional and dramatic humanitarian views, such as working whole-heartedly and intensely for a cause like global warming, animal rights, or any other cause where you immerse yourself in an organization devoted to over-arching change. You may express such views through political action or social service, or in a variety of other venues. The thrust of your desires and actions rests in humanitarian action, whether it's through charitable contributions, volunteerism, or direct employment within these realms of service. You might work for the Peace Corps or be an actor who is an activist for humanitarian causes. Either way, your purpose is to effect positive change in the world, and promote tolerance and compassion.

STAGE FOUR: If your Fourth Life Stage is guided by the 9 vibration, your work will tend to be more charitable in nature with plenty of opportunity to give much more of yourself. If you have done well financially in your life, you might be drawn to using your assets to finance programs and support causes you believe in. This is a time where you've mellowed and have developed a more caring and heart-felt attitude about yourself and about others than in earlier periods of your life.

Warning: If your 9 Life Stage is in your early years, this will be a rough period, full of losses and heavy challenges that bring early maturity. In the middle years, the 9 Life Stage is a time for integrating yourself with the higher principles of wisdom, self-less service, and giving back to the world. If you have saved your 9 Life Stage to the end, you are required to rise above the fray and become a humanitarian in whatever capacity you choose.

0 Challenge: The Cipher Number

THERE IS NO 9 CHALLENGE because 9 is the highest number. If your formula leads to a 9, then a 0 Challenge is substituted. In numerology, the 0 Challenge is called the Cipher Number. This number represents all or nothing, empty or full. You decide. With this number, you are given a "free pass," so to speak. You're being offered an enhanced dose of free will.

If you have a 0 Challenge, you can choose to amble idly along without a determined course or you can grab this profound opportunity to rise above your demons and achieve greatness. That is how powerful this energy can be for your Life Stage. To meet the challenge of the 0 vibration, you must have some sense of mastery over the constructive aspects of all the other numbers: independence, leadership, creativity, emotional self-expression, diplomacy, application and hard work, understanding, responsibility, wisdom, personal power, and humanitarian vision.

It's suggested that a person who has a 0 Challenge number on their journey is a well-traveled soul, so the 0 offers opportunities for the recipient to use his or her compilation of soul knowledge during his or her lifetime.

There's great opportunity for expansion and growth under this Challenge. The obstacles you face during a 0 challenge may not be many or they may be coming at you from all directions. You can think of it this way: This is the Challenge of Choice. Therefore, choice feels more confusing and difficult during this period. The 0 is challenging you to have the utmost faith in your own abilities to the extent that you can form a healthy sense of detachment with which you can analyze a situation, make a choice, and then act on that choice with ease and comfort, unconcerned and neutral in feeling regarding the outcome.

Warning: If you have a 0 Challenge in your life, it should not be taken lightly or cavalierly, because with this number, a decision must be made. We rarely make empowering choices by default. There is a lot of responsibility when any Life Stage contains a 0 Challenge. Use its energy wisely and fiercely.

Master Number Life Stages and Challenges

PRIMARILY, WHEN YOU EXPERIENCE a Master Number (11, 22, or 33) in one of your Life Stages, you are simply amplifying the energy of the 2, 4, or 6 accompanying it. If you upped the ante and have a Life Stage containing the higher vibration of the Master Number, you'll emphasize its metaphysical and spiritual elements. The destructive aspects of the Master Numbers are the same as the tendencies of their single-digit counterparts, only magnified by the Master vibration.

11/2 Life Stage

IF YOU'RE WORKING with the 11 energy, you're developing an extraordinary connection with your intuition and sensitivity. The pressure to wear your "psychic shield" will be at an all-time high under this Master Number since it creates quite a bit of volatility in the midst of enormous personal and spiritual growth. Optimally, the 11/2 Life Stage allows you to catapult yourself into a creative, intuitive, service-oriented realm in whatever capacity you desire. The 11 is a more artistic and creative vibration (as opposed to the 22) which favors outlets such as media work, music, art, dance, poetry or anything that involves a visionary and future-leaning focus.

Remember also that the influence felt with the 11 energy is somewhat philosophic in nature and ultimately connected with spiritual and metaphysical study and illumination. Therefore, you could feel compelled to work in the arenas of social reform, philosophy, or social welfare. You may also feel a bit detached from the day-to-day practicalities of the world. With the higher vibration presented by the number 11, you may feel a constant underlying sense of nervousness, tension or restlessness.

Warning: There is a chance for fame or being placed in the spotlight as a result of this Life Stage. This is a time for sudden and sometimes repeated changes in all realms of your life. If the 11 vibration is too intense, this Master Life Stage will feel more like a 2 energy to you. Either way, hyper-sensitivity is one of your primary and consistent challenges during this Life Stage.

11/2 Challenge

WHEN YOU HAVE the 11/2 Master Number as a Challenge (see page 111), you must respect the demands of the energy of both the numbers 11 and 2. You're being called to step up your vibration with the 11: to lead with spiritual clarity, purpose, and compassion. The lessons of the 2 call into play aspects related to partnership, relationship, service, and love. The challenge here is to have the strength, determination, and vision to operate in the constructive rather than the destructive aspects of those two numbers.

22/4 Life Stage

THIS LIFE STAGE IS UNCOMMON. It usually comes into play only after you have experienced two preceding Life Stages of 11/2. If you experience this Life Stage, you've opted for an especially dramatic or traumatic path in your life. Because of the prior 11/2 Life Stages you've lived through, you've been challenged to become a "master soul" or at least been called upon to work in a profound way on a higher spiritual path. Most likely you'll have undergone radical changes along the way. You may even have a physical or mental handicap or major health issue.

With the 22/4 Life Stage, with all of this experience up to this point, you have a chance to do something truly profound that will affect people on a wide-ranging scale. You'll build something of lasting value that will benefit humankind in a way that will keep giving even after you're gone. The 22/4 is the number that opens the door to high levels of personal and financial success if you utilize your incredible organizational skills to apply practical solutions to the problems encountered in the everyday world. This is a highly productive period of your life, yet also not easy considering it is chock-full of tests. Focus and endurance are a must.

Warning: Whether you like it or not, your actions set an example for others, so you must know that your actions speak louder than your words during a 22/4 Life Stage. Also it's a time where you need to be aware that you're subject to extreme sensitivity. You'll need to establish a balance between your personal life and your work life, as you tend to be a workaholic.

22/4 Challenge

NUMEROLOGISTS DO NOT LOOK at the 22/4 as a Challenge Number. The challenges of 22/4 are the same as for a 4 Challenge (see page 111).

33/6 Life Stage

THIS LIFE STAGE IS RARE and usually only present after you have two preceding Life Stages of 11/2 and 22/4. Because of what you've experienced during those prior Life Stages, you're on a path that demands that you operate with higher principles. Yours is not a conventional or smooth journey, yet your purpose is to use all of your experiences, easy and hard alike, to teach others and affect the world on a large scale.

This is an intense Life Stage where you're consistently offered opportunities to master your emotions and learn to think expansively both in terms of spirit and matter. This Life Stage will require a certain amount of self-sacrifice, yet the rewards are endless. Coupling the nurturing and visionary vibration of the 6 with the double expressive and communicative energy of the 3, you're a force for change, a teacher of teachers, and a person who shoulders great responsibility. With master energies, when operating optimally, you're protected and guided along the way.

33/6 Challenge

LIKE THE 22/4, THE 33/6 is not recognized as a Challenge Number. The primary challenges of the 33/6 are the same as with the 6 Life Stage, yet also this Master Number represents the test of healing yourself and others using spiritual principles.

If you haven't done so yet, please go back through the formulas now and calculate your own Life Stages and Challenges. Remember to download the *Redesign Your Life* workbook from FeliciaBender.com so you can fill out your personal Life Stages and Challenges to refer back to as you continue your "redesign your life" project.

PART THREE

YOUR
REDESIGN PROJECT

CHAPTER 5

STARTING YOUR REDESIGN PROJECT

NOW THAT YOU'VE DETERMINED your Life Path Number, figured out where you are in your Personal Year Cycle, and you have calculated your Life Stages and Challenges, it's time to put the puzzle pieces together in a way that supports the changes you want to make. In this chapter I'm going to outline a few case studies as examples of redecoration, remodeling, or renovation, adding Life Path-specific observations and components into the mix with the added tool of numerology. Your assignment is to focus on paring down your choices based on your Life Path Number.

The beauty of the Redesign Your Life system is that as you start to get a handle on the primary components of your Life Path, you can pinpoint your strengths, tendencies, obstacles, and overall sticking points. This tool allows us to narrow and anchor our focus on the core issues involved in making the changes we desire in a particular redesign project rather than getting lost in other extraneous issues that make us stray from our most effective route on our journey.

The key concept I'll be expanding on now is how to use your own Life Path mission as a *baseline* for the way you situate yourself in regard to the changes you want to make. By focusing squarely on your primary task at hand—as defined by your Life Path Number—you can come back to those key elements any time you begin to feel lost or overwhelmed.

Make sure you've got your Numbers handy in addition to the answers you gave to the questions in chapter 1, "Setting up Your Project." As you begin to further define your current redecoration, remodeling, or renovation project, keeping the key elements that define your Life Path right in front of you at all times can help you clear the road to make substantial, meaningful changes.

Developing Your Personal Blueprint for Change

THE BEST WAY TO WORK on your project is to ask yourself seven key questions:

1. What do I want to redecorate, remodel, or renovate in my life?
2. What are the main components of my Life Path mission?
3. How have my past decisions and actions, as they relate to my project, aligned or conflicted with my overarching Life Path mission?
4. How can I more closely align my decisions and actions, as they relate to my project, with my overarching Life Path mission?
5. What are my next three project-specific action items?

6. What is my time frame for accomplishing each action item?
7. How do I know when my action item is completed?

Let's take Tony as an example. A nineteen-year-old who just completed his first semester of college, Tony is a magnetic young man. He's an Eagle Scout, plays sports, and is popular with the girls. He also suffers from ADD and schoolwork hasn't been his forte. He did fine in high school, achieving a B average, so he thought he was doing okay during his first semester of college. Yet he never checked his grades throughout the term. He (and his parents) got a rude awakening when they discovered he had earned only a 0.75 GPA at the end of the first semester.

Looking at our seven key questions, let's see how Tony might define his redesign project for improving his performance in the second semester.

What do I want to redecorate, remodel or renovate in my life?
Tony feels certain that he needs to remodel his study habits. That becomes his project. He is being forced to reposition himself and come to an understanding of what's required of him in order to succeed in college and—by extension—in life. If he can't bring up his GPA substantially during the second semester of his freshman year, he'll be expelled from school. If that happens he'll be in an entirely different remodeling or renovation stage of his life.

What are the main components of my Life Path mission?
Tony is a 1 Life Path. Having chosen his project, he would go back and look at the section defining the key components of his Life Path in chapter 2. Here's what he could focus on.

- The 1 Life Path pertains to creativity, self-confidence, following

your unique voice, leadership, and ambition.
- The pesky obstacles a 1 Life Path can anticipate having to over-come include insecurity, addictive behaviors, and feelings of self-doubt, aggression, and self-importance.

Do my past decisions and actions, as they relate to my proj-ect, align or conflict with my overarching Life Path mission? Tony hasn't yet jumped on to the 1 Life Path bandwagon. Yet, let's be realistic: He's only 19. This is the perfect time for him to begin to take himself seriously and ask hard questions about his future. Tony doesn't know what he wants to major in yet, which is common among freshman. He has a couple of semesters until he's required to pin it down. Because of his ADD, he has difficul-ties with distraction. One of the things that is really distracting to him is his personal relationship. He has a girlfriend who attends another college, therefore he spends a lot of time texting her, talk-ing to her on the phone, and thinking about her.

In the past, Tony has gotten by easily on his charms, which are authentic and substantial. He's a really nice guy. But now that he's out in the "real world," he's got to figure out how to focus on his studies in a way that an academic environment demands. With his first semester report card he has been handed a reality check regarding his academic performance.

Tony hasn't been taking full responsibility for his studies.

How can I more closely align my decisions and actions, as they relate to my project, with my overarching Life Path mission? Having learned about his Life Path Number, Tony can make decisions based on his key strengths and be mindful of his inherent tendencies and obstacles. If Tony realizes at this young age that he's meant to be in a *leadership position* in his life, he can begin to focus on that aspect in everything he does. Tony can reposition himself to begin to make decisions for his education, and by extension his future career path, that are more in alignment with his 1 Life Path goals of cultivating creativity and confidence in everything he does.

If he starts looking at himself and his study habits with his 1 Life Path as his lens, he can realize that he was attracted to being an Eagle Scout for a reason. He can reflect on the ways in which he's taken charge in his life—of himself and of others—and check in with himself regarding how he felt when he was accomplishing these tasks and activities that were in alignment with his mission of developing leadership skills. I'll bet money that these are the times when Tony felt the best about himself. These are the moments in the past during which he felt empowered and energized.

Alternately, as he begins to look at his life with his 1 Life Path lens, he can also realize that he felt the worst when he was acting on the more destructive elements of his Life Path mission, such as feeling like a victim, not behaving responsibly, or feeling "holier than thou" and had a chip on his shoulder. As he learns the guiding forces behind his Life Path mission, Tony can start to consolidate lessons from his experiences in a way that can help him define positive parameters for his lifestyle and make good choices about his college career and moving forward in his life.

Tony can start by opening up to the idea that his life is at its optimal when he's independent, acting on original ideas, and using focused concentration and determination to achieve what he wants. When he begins to understand that he's going to feel a sense of validation and alignment with himself in a way he hasn't felt before when he starts to step up to the plate and take control of his life, Tony will be able to make great use of his 1 Life Path tool. Only when he consciously becomes a star pupil in the School of Hard Knocks of life will Tony come to see his true power. I'm not suggesting that 1 Life Path's have substandard lives, just pointing out that the 1 vibration brings a level of difficulty that has to do with learning resilience through challenging and difficult experiences.

To commence his life redesign project, Tony must come to terms with the ways that he avoids taking responsibility and direction in certain parts of his life. He's starting to see that when he sidesteps problems and doesn't stay on top of things in his life (like reading assignments and writing papers), he always suffers. He rarely has a positive outcome when he isn't taking a leadership role in his own life. When he's working in the more destructive realm of his Life Path, he lets others, such as his college buddies and his girlfriend, take the helm; those actions always result in a personal train wreck.

Let's say one of the reasons Tony was attracted to his girlfriend is that she's highly ambitious, intelligent, and a go-getter. He thought being with her would allow him to coast along without having to take much initiative himself. What he didn't understand was that if he wants a successful relationship with a partner who's "going somewhere" in life, he needs to take inspiration from her and step up his own game. A 1 Life Path is all about taking initiative, so whenever Tony is just drifting along, he's not stepping up to his 1 Life Path mission.

Of course, with Tony, his remodeling project has two basic components. His primary goal in remodeling his life is to restructure his study habits. Yet, in digging deep into where he was and was not in alignment with his Life Path Number, he realized that he also needed to remodel his relationship with his girlfriend. Another way you could say this is that he needed to begin to remodel the way and the reason why he chooses his partners.

What are my next three project-specific action items? At the end of the evaluation process, Tony's action items might look like this:

1. *To check my grades on each exam and each homework assignment as soon as they're available from the professor so that I can know what my grades are and not be surprised at the end of the semester.* Remember that Tony is a happy-go-lucky guy who was surprised he failed his classes during the first semester because he wasn't following up at all on the results of his homework and exams. Here he's pledging to face the music up front and follow up as soon as the results are available to him.

2. *To turn off my cell phone, TV, and iPod (and any other electronic device) when I am studying.* This is a key element for Tony! For those of us who remember typing on an actual typewriter, listening to LPs on a record player, and making phone calls on a landline, this issue might sound silly or easily overcome. Yet for Gen Yers, electronics are a major issue. Okay, to be fair, this can be an issue for people of all ages. So while it sounds simple just to "turn off the noise," it's a major decision for Tony.

3. *To decide if I want to have a girlfriend right now.* Tony needs to establish his priorities. He and his girlfriend have a long distance relationship that's difficult to maintain. Tony is very distracted by their constant texting, calls, weekend visits, and daydreaming about her during her absences. These distractions didn't cause him to fail his classes, but they certainly contributed. Tony's last action item is to make up his mind—and stick with his decision—to focus on his class work and put his dating life on the back burner for now.

What is my time frame for accomplishing each action item?
Tony's action items are fairly consolidated with a three-month
(one semester) time-frame.

How do I know when my action item is completed? He'll
know at the end of the semester if he's been successful in working
with and following through on his action items.

Given Tony's young age, he's just beginning to tackle his 1
Life Path mission. He has to forge his way with a clear sense of
confidence while following the beat of his own drummer. Already
he's experienced something common to a 1 Life Path: a seriously
uncomfortable awakening having to do with his failure to be a
decisive and dynamic force in his own life.

What I have observed through my own personal experiences
and by consulting with different clients is this: Experience is not
only the *best* teacher, it's the *only* teacher. Surely a guy like Tony—
and like most of us—wouldn't shake things up unless it were a crisis situation. The only way he can "get it" is by going through these
challenging experiences on his own.

The Rule of Three

BREAKING DOWN YOUR PROJECT into small, manageable
"bites" will enable you to move forward when you might otherwise hover in indecision or mental paralysis. The Rule of Three is:
Always define three clear actions you can take to get to your goal.
Even if these action items seem "easy," write them down. As you
accomplish them, check them off your list.

Once you've completed your first three tasks, formulate three
more action items. Do those and then invent three more. Keep

taking new action steps until you reach your life redesign goal.

Trust me, this one simple rule will help you accomplish everything from the smallest to the most monumental changes you want to make.

Clearing Your Physical and Emotional Clutter

ONE OF THE CONSISTENT and persistent challenges as you redecorate, remodel, and renovate will be learning to understand what's cluttering your life. The redesign process requires that you evaluate what your personal clutter looks and feels like, where it comes from, and how to sift through it. This means physical and environmental clutter, emotional clutter, and relationship clutter. You name it. Look at anything that is cluttering your life. The beginning of a redesign project is the time to focus on letting go of anything that is no longer needed. This way you can make space for change to enter.

As you become intimately familiar with the three tools of numerology we're using, you can begin to hone in on how your different clumps of clutter operate, particularly as clutter pertains to your emotions. Behavioral change needs to be made when you are not in alignment with your Life Path mission.

You can't watch an episode of *Hoarders* without realizing that the massive material clutter the participants are living in is the direct result of their scarred emotional lives. Likewise, every popular weight-loss television program unearths its participants' buried emotional issues at the core of their weight issues—whether these are the residuals of abuse or trauma, or simply represent the way someone processes stressful events and uncomfortable thoughts and feelings. How you manifest emotional clutter is a barrier to living your optimal life.

207

As you start your redesign project, you're going to come face to face with some of the ways you have chosen to clutter your life, be it with objects you collect, negative beliefs, haunting memories, or unresolved relationships. The good news is that once you step back and see your clutter for what it is, you can begin to do something about it.

The key here is this: When you view your issues from a healthy distance, you can begin to lessen the hooks they place in you and come to recognize your triggers. The bonus you get by knowing your Life Path mission is that you can use the information to help you locate and minimize the clutter that's holding you back from living your optimal lifestyle. Your emotional clutter will most often reflect the destructive tendencies inherent in your Life Path Number.

As I prepared to write this chapter, I felt the need to clear my own physical clutter. Before I could begin to write lucid sentences, I cleaned out my email inbox and organized my desk. I even dusted. When my office was neatly organized, my thoughts flowed more freely and I could focus on the task at hand. You know how that is. When the laundry's piled high, the toilets need to be cleaned, and the dishes are stacking up in the sink it's next to impossible to feel calm, energized, focused, and creative. Cleaning your house and organizing your physical surroundings works wonders for your mental clarity. So the first step to redesigning your life has to do with getting your house in order—literally.

Next on your docket is clearing your emotional clutter. This must be an ongoing task.

Do you ever wonder how the heck the coffee table collected so much dust in one week when nobody ever goes into that room? Clearing your emotional clutter is rather like dusting your coffee table. You have to do it consistently or there will be buildup.

Are you an emotional hoarder, holding on to every fragment of garbage that should have been composted a long time ago? If you chuck garbage into the compost pile, it can mature into rich fertilizer. If you leave it hanging around, it just rots into a smelly, moldy mess. You can say the same about your emotional clutter.

Of course, it's often easier said than done to get rid of emotional garbage effectively. The first step toward emotional health is to *realize that you have some clutter* and need help finding the right tools to start cleaning it up.

Please understand: *Everyone* has emotional clutter. So give yourself a break. Even the person you think has every little thing together experiences plenty of emotional turmoil.

When you focus on the major forces at work in your life as outlined by your Life Path Number, your thinking about your relationships may undergo a profound shift. I've seen what I'd call turbo-shifts happen for clients, where it's like a light bulb has turned on and they're able to fill in a mysterious gap of meaning about a relationship or finally find the explanation that they've been longing for as to why someone in their life behaved as he or she did. At that moment, their emotional clutter gets a major "Hoovering"!

I had a 2 Life Path client once who had experienced terrible hurt feelings from what she felt was rejection from her family. When she saw that part of her Life Path mission had to do with being overly sensitive and with desperately needing unconditional love (among other things), she was miraculously able to relinquish the grip of agony she'd held on to for so long about her disappointment in herself and also in the way in which her family didn't meet her needs. The simple tool of knowing the details of her Life Path mission was enough to offer her a profound shift in the way she perceived her past and present relationships. That helped her clean up her emotional clutter in regard to her family. Certainly, her revelation didn't make her relationship with her family suddenly change into "sparkles and unicorns," yet she was able to use her new 2 Life Path lens to view her situation from a different perspective.

The Fear Factor

YOU KNOW YOUR LIFE PATH NUMBER. You see yourself in its reflective surface. You're able to recognize what this *optimal you* might look and feel like. You totally relate to your tendencies and obstacles and can see how you've integrated many of these aspects of your Life Path into your daily existence. You've located what you want to redecorate, remodel, or renovate in your life. You've answered the seven Redesign Your Life questions and punched out some action items. "So, what's the deal?" you're asking yourself. "Why are the muscles in my chest clenched?" or (choose all that apply):

- "Why can't I move forward with this in the way I imagined?"
- "Why did I just get a call that my friend was in a car accident and needs help?"
- "Why did my dog just die?"
- "Why did I just get a bladder infection?"
- "Why did I just lose my job?"
- "Why did my kid just get arrested?"

Yes. When we set our intentions upon redesigning our lives, oftentimes the Universe wants to test our resolve. "Just making sure you really want it!" is what it seems to be saying.

This is exactly the juncture when the fear factor stares you down. This happens particularly when you've started your project and are really making headway. You're expanding into this new you and then ... *slap*.

The reason I bring this up is because I want you to expect this to happen. Rather than being taken by surprise, I want you to fortify yourself and be ready for the confrontation. Wear your strongest set of armor. Remind yourself of your powerful intentions. Give yourself permission to make some people angry or uncomfortable as you recalibrate your actions and grow into the optimal you. A friend of mine often quotes Oprah Winfrey's comment: "Whatever you fear most has no power—it's your *fear* that has the power." My friend adds: "Fear is either a reflection of your past experiences or a worry about the future. Stay present in this moment and rejoice for all that is great in it."

Here's an analogy. When you begin to physically exercise, you push yourself. You understand that when you feel a sense of pain, that is actually the *goal* of exercising. If you're in a painless comfort zone, you're really not changing your body. If you stick with your exercise program, you begin to actually *seek* ways to keep surprising your body so that it'll continue to strengthen. You do so because *it feels good* and you're getting results from your consistency. Not only do your muscles get stronger, but because of the bursts of serotonin excreted by your body when you exercise your heart gains stamina and strength, you lose weight, gain muscle, and your mood improves. You get to the point where a slight amount of soreness *is your norm*. You know you're training effectively if you "feel it" the next day—not to the point of being so sore you can't move, yet being sore enough to notice you accomplished something.

The same can be said as you wrestle with your personal fears: The more you saddle up and ride them, the less terrifying they seem. It's good to embrace the perspective that a bit of fear means you're moving forward and making important changes. I know folks who are afraid of pain, afraid of being alone, afraid of heights, afraid of being talked about behind their backs. There are certainly multiple levels of fear with which we may contend daily. Yet if you challenge yourself by moving through your fear in increments, the chances that the power your fear held over you can begin to dissipate, if not disappear altogether.

Fears always come into play when we're making significant changes. *Always.* The trick is to reposition yourself with the "shield" that knowledge of your Life Path brings to you.

Have you ever had the experience where you revisited something later in life that you were afraid of as a child only to discover how benign it was? I have. When I was a kid, we had a book about Johnny Appleseed. It was a "young reader" book with few illustrations. Yet there was one drawing at the end of the book of Johnny Appleseed as an old man that scared the bejeezus out of me. No kidding. I had nightmares about that pencil drawing for a long time. I went back home as an adult and my mother asked me to clear out some boxes from storage and—lo and behold—there was the book.

Even as an adult, my heart raced at the memory of that horrible picture that frightened me so much. I had to steady myself as I turned to the end of the book to look at the picture. There it was. The same picture that had haunted me was staring me in the face. Yet it was just a pencil drawing of a man that looked like a dried apple doll. It was so crazy to me that something as simple as that picture could have incited such fearful power over me as a child.

The same can be said for any fearful "thing" that keeps you from expanding yourself in a direction you want to go. This can be accomplished with something as silly as the Johnny Appleseed drawing in the children's book to your response to your abusive former husband or wife. Acknowledging your personal fear factor is also a great way to begin to unravel the ways in which you construct your fears and participate in their perpetuation.

One of the interesting thoughts that stand in the way of many people when they're attempting to redesign their lives has to do with their beliefs. Perhaps you would say: "It's not fair that I don't make enough money." You might also say: "I've just always been this way. I don't care about money. I just want to do my art." If so, the belief you're working with has to do with your belief that art and commerce are mutually exclusive. Your financial lack has to do with parallel desires: You want money, but you don't care about it. It's really no wonder you have money issues, considering you're giving yourself mixed messages about how money fits into your life.

I have always been artistic and creative. Early on in my life, the idea of knowing anything about contracts, finances, or business seemed ridiculous to me. It was a-okay with me that my husband took care of all the finances. Anything dealing with money seemed boring and uninteresting. I thought it just wasn't "me." Yet I have since discovered that this belief just wasn't true. When I was challenged with the need to take care of myself, I stepped up and got interested in how the material world operates. Then I decided to participate in it. I got a real estate license and immersed myself in understanding how contracts work, how financing and loans operate, and how to elevate my own credit rating.

And I discovered managing money was fun after all; fun insofar as I was able to derive deep satisfaction and empowerment by learning how to be smart about my financial life rather than a victim of my own circumstances. Do you know what? My *fear* of not being able to take care of myself and my children turned out to be the very thing that propelled me to focus on my finances and become tenacious about achieving my goals.

As you peel away the layers of your different fears and limiting beliefs about what you're capable of doing based on your Life Path information, you have an opportunity to question the way you've constructed your reality up until this point. As you investigate the optimal components of your Life Path and recognize the symptoms when you're overactive or underactive with your Life Path characteristics, you can begin to see some of the ways you have limited yourself by *identifying* with the destructive aspects of your Life Path mission. To redesign your life effectively, you have a running start to work with your fears and dismantle their power over you.

The Commitment Factor

HOW COMMITTED ARE YOU to the outcome you're seeking? How committed are you to making changes? Change is a sticking point for most of us.

When working with clients, I've found one of the major issues everyone comes to the table with is commitment. There are two kinds. The first kind of commitment is the commitment it takes to complete the actions involved in achieving your redecoration, remodeling, or renovation project. It's easy to start something with exuberance and then, when the going gets tough or inconvenient, leave an action by the wayside. It's easy to fall back into old habits and come up with reasons or excuses why your project needs to be placed on hold or abandoned.

The second form of commitment holds a powerful grip on people's lives. It's actually a detrimental commitment, a commitment to *your story*. We've all constructed a story about ourselves based in our past experiences, relationships, and perceptions. Certain aspects of your story hold you back, tethering you to the box you've built around your life that limits you.

For instance, there's the Scarlett O'Hara complex: "I'll never go hungry again!" I know many older folks who built their entire lives around this story because they grew up during the Depression, and yet there are plenty of people of all ages who are committed to their vice grip on a particular story of suffering. The commitment to a story of lack drives them to make most of their choices in life based around fear of scarcity, even though the one time they had to steal a loaf of bread from a store to feed their family when they were ten years old happened decades ago. Since then, they've never been met with the reality of starvation or homelessness, yet internally, they feel it's on the verge of happening again. Rather than ousting that traumatic moment from their memory banks and replacing it with memories of the umpteen years they've been living well and without hunger, the "Scarlet O'Hara" continues to react as a scared, angry, hungry, fearful kid.

The lesson here is this concept: Our lives are comprised of our experiences. That's how it works. These aren't new ideas by any means. The key shift that needs to take place as you work with your Life Path Number to find the best avenue to redesign your life is to allow your life experiences to *inform* your current decisions, *not to control them!*

I know what I'm suggesting here is really difficult in practice. It's also something that isn't ever truly mastered. None of us can achieve this feat 100 percent of the time. Yet if you keep this idea in front of you, it's a powerful tool in your redesign toolkit.

When I was working intensely with clients doing pranic healing®—a form of energy healing I did with people for several years in private practice—I was disconcerted to discover the number of women who came for healing sessions who had been sexually abused or raped. Literally three out of every five women I worked with ended up sharing this type of memory with me. Many times, much of their physical problems and emotional issues had a locus in abuse. Some were molested repeatedly as children by a family member. One was violently raped in front of her six-year old son by a man who broke into her apartment. These were not stories for the faint-hearted.

One of the questions I grappled with over and over again as I was working with such a woman was: Can she heal from this trauma? And if she can, *how?*

I remember a profound breakthrough in my own thinking about this hard question. I was taking a class with a wonderful instructor who is a medical intuitive. She shared her personal story of being sexually abused when she was growing up. She spoke eloquently about her own process with the trauma and how it had governed her life for years until she made a conscious and concerted decision to forgive her perpetrator. Yes, *forgive.*

I squirmed in my seat. "Forgive?" I thought. "But what about this horrible violation? What about the fact that this was done to a *child?*" I just couldn't wrap my brain around how even to begin to forgive such a person.

Then she said, "By forgiving my perpetrator, I was able to completely let go of the power and control he was exerting over my life. Even though I was raped several times by this man, it was as though he was raping me every single day of the rest of my life—all day, every day. When I was able to forgive him, I was able to let go of the power and control this absolutely powerless man was yielding over me."

She went on to add the essential tool for forgiveness. "When I say I forgave him, I mean I was able to forgive yet *not condone.* To me, to forgive means to *let go of the person* in order to sever my traumatic connection with them. We're always really hung up on the idea that if we forgive someone it erases or puts a stamp of approval on their actions. This isn't the case! *The act of forgiveness does not include condoning the behavior.* Only by forgiving was I able to walk away and begin to live my own life, a life where I wasn't a rape victim every day."

While this is a dramatic example, the idea here is extremely powerful to consider in letting go of negative aspects of your story as you move into remodeling or renovating your life.

You must come to terms with your level of commitment to your own painful story and be realistic about how willing you are to let go of portions of it as you dig deeper into your project. This extends even to the smaller emotional commitments.

I can speak for myself: sometimes I'm in an agitated mood and I'm committed to it. I won't budge. Then you know what happens? The day goes awry and proves to me that my foul mood was right on the money. Everything that happens during the day when I'm committed to my bad mood will prove to me that I'm right: all drivers that day are stupid, my partner is insensitive, my kids are a mess, and the sky is falling. Then I'll stub my toe. Or lock my keys in the car. Or lose my phone. Or whatever else will prove to me that there's plenty to be mad about. It's the law of attraction: My bad mood attracts more of the same.

If I can shift my mood—even if I feel I have something legitimate to complain about—it's amazing how I attract better things throughout the day. And if another challenge is thrown my way, I'm much more likely to handle it well rather than disintegrate because of it.

Follow-through and Momentum

LET'S GO BACK TO THE FIRST KIND of commitment: the positive commitment to our chosen actions. Another sticking point in enacting any real change in your life has to do with follow-though and momentum. Your project will require that you commit to the change you want to make and work steadily to achieve it. Taking small "bites" out of a project is really handy. By allowing yourself to take small, incremental steps toward your proposed accomplishment, the likelihood that you'll follow-through to completion is high.

217

You'll finish it without delays and just in time to start another worthwhile project.

Knowing your Life Path can help you create a blueprint for change that is sufficiently meaningful to impel you to action even when life tosses you a curve ball, as Bryon's story shows. Bryon is fifty-five years old and has lived a rather amazing 5 Path life.

The child of artists, Bryon lived a vagabond existence as a child, moving from place to place with his "hippie" parents and his brother. He thrived in the atmosphere of change and creativity in his parents' household and was allowed a lot of freedom to do as he pleased. From the get-go, Bryon was the epitome of the "fearless adventurer." As he grew into his teens, however, Bryon couldn't live hard enough or fast enough. He started with alcohol and amphetamines. As addictions began to overtake his life, he spiraled into chaos and irresponsibility.

Bryon's life went through a rocky three-year-long transformation in his twenties. During his first Saturn Return when he was twenty-nine (which was also a 5 Personal Year for him, doubling up his already intense 5 Life Path energy), he hit "rock bottom" and checked into rehab. Shortly after becoming clean and sober, Bryon met his wife-to-be at an Alcoholics Anonymous meeting. As unlikely as it may sound, given the timing of their meeting early in Bryon's sobriety, they formed a solid, healthy relationship. Today they're still happily married.

In his thirties, Bryon started his own business in the travel industry, leading tours for groups of people to a variety of exotic destinations. He took up photography and produced amazing travel photographs. He adopted his wife's daughter and loved being a supportive father.

During Bryon's last 9 Personal Year, he was given a diagnosis of Parkinson's disease. While only in the beginning stages, the disease started to impede his movement and caused him to feel fatigued. He was angry at this sudden turn of fate and lashed out at himself and sometimes at those around him. He and his wife considered separation.

Bryon continued to struggle with the progression of the disease. He took a hiatus from his travel business and focused on his health. He researched the disease and took action to get the best medical help and support.

Three years into the disease, Bryon had a remarkable experience, which he describes like this: "One day, I just stopped. I stopped feeling sorry for myself. I stopped wondering, 'Why me?' and instead started living. I started to truly understand that this *is* me. *This is the new me.* And I'm just as much *me* right now as I was *me* before now. I felt this huge weight lift from me as I embraced the fact that this is my reality and so, now what am I going to do with it?"

Following that day, Bryon found new medications that stopped his body from shaking and allow him to walk with greater ease and even to play golf! Even though the medication is working well right now, Bryon knows that his condition will continue to challenge him and his doctor's with balancing the right kinds of medicines and dosages. The medications have other effects on him that Bryon has had to negotiate. And yet he's now inspired and grateful every day that he can get up and contribute to someone or something during the day.

Bryon is learning to be the "poster child" of his vibrant 5 Life Path energy. He's developing freedom and discipline in the most profound ways. Simultaneously he's being called to step up to be an inspiration and example to others by keeping his sense of fearless adventurousness in the face of the potentially debilitating condition that will eventually erode his physical abilities. This is requiring him to develop a tremendous sense of courage and confidence.

I love looking at Bryon's life from the perspective of the 5 Life

Path. He's lived it all: fearlessness, adventure, addictions, lots of freedom, and then a demand for a reinvention that encompasses all of it.

I'd like to show you how you might begin to use Life Path information in a practical way. I want to stress the fact that you can do all kinds of different jobs and achieve all kinds of different things no matter what your Life Path Number might be. Every person's Life Path can hold a similar type of experience as another. You bring to it your uniqueness, your own specific talents and interests, and you wrap it all up in the influences that are specific to your life. The key is to be able to extract the meaning or core issue of that experience in the context of the elements of your Life Path. The Life Path Number helps you know when you're working optimally and when you're overactive or underactive.

Let's do a "for instance." I'm going to take a question submitted to Dr. Phil's advice column in the January 2012 issue of *O Magazine*, and then provide examples of how you might look at the proposed issue from different angles depending on the Life Path Number of the person who wrote the question. Here's the question:

> *"I start projects without finishing them. It happens with everything from painting a room to looking for a job. I set out with so much motivation, but I can't maintain it, and then I just stop. I have a lovely wife who often picks up my slack… My life has always been this way: I dig myself into a hole, and someone steps in to help me."*

Here's how you might break this down in the light of different Life Path traits, tendencies, and obstacles. Let's review the issues and pretend the questioner's name is David. David starts projects without finishing them. He begins them with a bang, yet lacks follow-through and rarely reaches completion. Everyone from his mother to his wife enables him to underperform.

220

1 Life Path

IF DAVID HAS A 1 LIFE PATH, he's being challenged with the destructive tendencies of his path. He's meant to act with creativity and confidence in all he does. Optimally, David would take a leadership role in his work and his personal life. He would be driven toward success and be an independent thinker. David is defaulting into the underactive tendencies of the 1 Life Path. He's always struggled with dependence on others. He's insecure and rather helpless. David needs to recognize he's meant to be a leader and work through his strong sense of insecurity.

2 Life Path

IF DAVID HAS A 2 LIFE PATH, he's been living in the more underactive aspects of his path. Since 2 Life Path energy is all about giving and receiving love, harmony, balance, and being of service in some way that is meaningful, optimally David would be a loving and appreciative husband. When 2 Life Path people aren't stepping up to plate, they can be victims and hand over their power to others. They want approval from those around them. Even though he might be trying to please, as someone with a 2 Life Path, David's oversensitivity is probably stopping him from following through with his projects because of his fear of failure or rejection.

3 Life Path

IF DAVID HAS A 3 LIFE PATH, he's certainly working in the overactive aspects of his path. David's life is all about creative expression and communication, yet he doesn't appear to have gotten a handle on these gifts yet. Instead, he's scattered and lacks follow-through. Chances are good that David is full of creative ideas that come at him so quickly and frequently that he can't possibly complete all of them. Since the 3 Life Path is about lightness and fun, he's been happy to allow the people around him to manage the more serious parts of his life rather than being responsible for them himself.

4 Life Path

IF DAVID HAS A 4 LIFE PATH, he's leaning way over into the underactive side of his path. As a person with a 4 Life Path, he's meant to be dependable, trustworthy, detail oriented, practical, and a problem solver. David doesn't appear to display any of those 4 Life Path characteristics. David's task as a person with a 4 Life Path is to come to terms with the fact that he'll feel much more on target and satisfied with his life when he decides to take on more responsibility, which includes following through with stability and embracing the process.

5 Life Path

IF DAVID HAS A 5 LIFE PATH, he's sliding over into the overactive aspects of his path. The 5 Life Path is all about creating freedom through self-discipline. A 5 Life Path will also struggle with a need to be really independent, doing what they want whenever they want to, and then swing over into the opposite and become extremely dependent on others and unable to care for themselves effectively. David's been enabled by those around him to dip into the destructive tendencies of his Life Path mission. David will feel better when he can discipline himself to finish tasks while remaining his freedom-loving self.

6 Life Path

IF DAVID HAS A 6 LIFE PATH, he's operating in the overactive tendencies that the 6 vibration brings with it. David is meant to be a wonderful nurturer, which would mean that it's important for him to be successful at providing for his family. Given that his wife pinch hits for him all the time and takes up the slack for his inability to complete even the most basic tasks, David is being over taken by the destructive elements of his 6 vibration. The person with a 6 Life Path is a visionary and a perfectionist. Perhaps David doesn't finish anything due to an overweening need to be perfect. If he finishes something, more than likely it won't be perfect because, after all, perfection is an illusion. If he doesn't finish, there's nothing tangible to critique.

7 Life Path

IF DAVID HAS A 7 LIFE PATH, he's working in the underactive elements of his path. Having a 7 Life Path, optimally David is thorough, studious, and diligent (if not a bit obsessive). The fact that he can't follow through on anything and has those around him take up the slack for him is a default position for a 7 Life Path. The 7 Life Path is all about intuition and intellectual analysis, so perhaps David just isn't interested in painting a room and should learn to tell his wife up front that he'd rather hire someone else to do it.

8 Life Path

IF DAVID HAS AN 8 LIFE PATH, he's operating in the underactive energies of the number 8. As a person with an 8 Life Path, David is meant to be a powerhouse, a force to be reckoned with. He's meant to act with heartfelt power and authority. David's 8 energy also demands that he step up and use his skills if he wants to be financially abundant. Instead, David has defaulted into passivity; he is giving away his personal power. Being able to complete projects successfully would be a good first step for David. As he begins to own his own power, even in modest ways, he'll understand that his mission is to develop power and abundance in every aspect of his life.

9 Life Path

IF DAVID HAS A 9 LIFE PATH, he's acting on the underactive aspects of his energy. Having a 9 Life Path, David's primary mission is to develop integrity and wisdom in everything he does. David isn't participating in his life enough to finish anything he starts. By being submissive and perceiving himself as a victim, he's working with the underactive 9 energy. Optimally, David would be at his best if he were leading by example and offering himself and those around him the best things that life has to offer. David needs to come to understand that he's at his best when he's reliable and working to help others as well as himself.

These preceding nine descriptions are brief examples of how you can utilize the information provided by your Life Path Number. While we can all find ourselves with similar issues as David, the angle that we go about working with it can vary greatly from Life Path Number to Life Path Number. When you can locate the key aspects of your own optimal self, you can throw a tight lasso around the core of your problem, and then make more focused headway in your efforts to create change.

The following reference guide outlines the optimal, overactive, and underactive qualities of the different Life Path Numbers.

Use it to calibrate the changes you want to make with your redecoration, remodeling, or renovation project. In the next chapter we'll focus on how to add the tools of the Personal Year Cycle and Life Stages and Challenges into your blueprint.

LIFE PATH NUMBER "CHEAT SHEET"

1 Life Path

The 1 Life Path is connected with: new opportunity, inspiration, new starts, initiation, standing alone, originality, courage, concentration, determination, and leadership.

Optimal: energetic, bold, forward looking, persistent, initiatory, confident, ambitious, self-reliant, optimistic, synergetic, and problem solving.

Overactive: impatient, self-important, intolerant, unyielding, defiant, headstrong, arrogant, greedy, possessive, dictatorial, addicted, and domineering.

Underactive: dependent, insecure, helpless, victimized, passive, weak willed, lacking self-respect, wishy-washy, and cowardly.

2 Life Path

The 2 Life Path is connected with: sensitivity, teamwork, cooperation, receptivity, tolerance, partnerships, details, friendships, harmony, and gradual growth.

Optimal: flexible, helpful, receptive, courteous, intuitive, supportive, warm, insightful, peacemaking, diplomatic, loving, and emotionally available.

Overactive: manipulative, fault finding, resentful, resisting, devious, disapproving, condescending, interfering, self-serving, and narrow minded.

Underactive: self-deprecating, indecisive, uncaring, self-centered, dependent, inactive, overly sensitive, and unresponsive.

3 Life Path

The 3 Life Path is connected with: pleasure, self-improvement, laughter, sexual expression, artistic creativity, communication, writing, happy times, quick recoveries, easy money, instability, and dramatic emotional ups and downs.

Optimal: literary talent, cultivated, amusing, witty, well-liked, magnetic, optimistic, inspiring, authentic emotional expression, inventive, imaginative, artistic, and intelligent.

Overactive: scattered, over-confident, gossipy, superficial, exaggerating, lacking concentration, difficulty with follow through, emotionally volatile, and irresponsible.

Underactive: depressed, jealous, self-doubting, inarticulate, unthinking, indecisive, bored, petty, temperamental, insincere, unenthusiastic, and fearful.

4 Life Path

The 4 Life Path is connected with: material interests, structure, managing finances, creating lasting foundations, hard work, stable finances, solid management, organization, efficiency, physical activity, limitations.

Optimal: dependable, reliable, thrifty, methodical, analytical, productive, solid, cautious, disciplined, sensible, loyal, trustworthy, and persevering.

Overactive: rigid, narrow minded, worrisome, inflexible, dreary, emotionally numb, uncompromising, provincial, blunt, and lost in detail.

Underactive: disorganized, apathetic, sarcastic, impractical, careless, inefficient, distracted, idle, and neglectful.

5 Life Path

The 5 Life Path is connected with: promotion, sensuality, sales, sex, freedom, travel, communication, changes, fluctuation, flexibility, excitement, and adventure.

Optimal: reliable, innovative, daring, charming, sets healthy boundaries, forward thinking, charming, curious, adaptable, independent, clever, and resourceful.

Overactive: indulgent, reckless, abandons relationships too soon, impatient, thrill seeking, erratic, extremely independent, insatiable, restless, easily overwhelmed, addicted, and highly emotional.

Underactive: fearful of change, stagnant, dependent, conforming, fearful of freedom, dull, ineffective, procrastination, emotionally volatile, and depressive.

6 Life Path

The 6 Life Path is connected with: home, family, relationships, marriage, divorce, romance, responsibility, friendships, emotions, deliberation, harmony, teaching, and justice..

Balanced: home loving, advisory, friendly, tolerant, supportive, responsible, appreciative, peace making, protective, devoted, loving, stable, and sensible.

Overactive: distortedly idealistic, critical, interfering, opinionated, possessive, stubborn, sacrificing, martyred, unreasonable, obstinate, unforgiving, disheartened, slavish, and self-righteous.

Underactive: uncaring, uncooperative, biased, unconcerned, indulgent, lacking energy, unwelcoming, and non-committal.

7 Life Path

The 7 Life Path is connected to: mysticism, intuition, inner growth, examination, study, analysis, reflection, mental acuity, planning, unsolicited help, specialization, philosophy, solitude, and refinement.

Balanced: tolerant, thorough, diligent, intellectual, intuitive, analytical, perceptive, scientific, exact, meditative, mystical, expert, bookish, poised, telepathic, instinctive, truth seeking, studious, and wise.

Overactive: fearful, nervous, critical, obsessive, paranoid, indecisive, secretive, emotionally repressed, distrustful, guarded, intimidating, evasive, self-conscious, perfectionist, and pessimistic.

Underactive: superficial, naïve, ignorant, overly trusting, introverted, empty headed, superficial, faithless, undeveloped, uninformed, and unsure.

8 Life Path

The 8 Life Path is connected to: influence, money, action, business success, business failure, control, material objects, status, loss, gain, executive administration, management, ego, leadership, and personal power.

Balanced: prosperous, entrepreneurial, realistic, planner, commanding, self-confident, persuasive, ambitious, businesslike, clear-headed, disciplined, honorable, ethical, and enterprising.

Overactive: abusive of power, egotistical, scheming, aggressive, materialistic, corrupt, demanding, domineering, preoccupied with power and money, unsympathetic, overly ambitious, confrontational, greedy, too forceful, and rebellious.

Underactive: passive, vulnerable, fearful, insecure, avoiding of power and money, poor judgment, powerless, and shortsighted.

9 Life Path

The 9 Life Path is connected to: unconditional love, humanitarianism, reward, leadership by example, dramatic endings, emotional love, emotional crisis, the finer things in life, conclusions, deep love, compassion, magnetism, travel, idealism, charity, artistry, creativity, spirituality, romance, and forgiveness.

Balanced: artistic, philanthropic, affectionate, creative, forgiving, passionate, benevolent, warm, tolerant, sentimental, loving, generous, idealistic, romantic, open minded, enthusiastic, trustworthy, hospitable, and humane.

Overactive: deceiving, self-centered, lacking integrity, overly emotional, prejudiced, resentful, presenting a bad example, irresolute, vindictive, hateful, and hostile.

Underactive: close minded, impersonal, arrogant, aloof, distant, unemotional, elusive, submissive, drifting, fainthearted, victimized, lost, and lazy.

229

CHAPTER 6

REFINING YOUR BLUEPRINT
FOR TRANSFORMATION

KNOWING KEY COMPONENTS of your numerology is a great way to continue to evolve into the next phase of your life. I trust you can also see how your evolution during your lifetime is an intricate and ongoing experience; full of luscious surprises and painful challenges. By now I trust you have more than a basic sense of how to incorporate your Life Path Number into the way you think about your life redecoration, remodeling, or renovation project. One of the ways to refine your blueprint for transformation is to add what you know about your Personal Year Cycles and your Life Stages and Challenges into the mix. In this chapter we'll discuss how to use these additional numerological tools to plan out the specific details of your project.

Using the Personal Year Cycle

THERE ARE MULTIPLE REASONS why knowing your Personal Year Cycle is useful. Everyone feels a strong sense of change and shifting energies at the end of the calendar year. The franticness of the winter holidays and New Year's Eve festivities may be the vehicle we use to explain it. Yet each year actually does bring us something unique: the vibration of a new number. It's important how we choose to participate in each year of our lives. In this chapter, I am going to show you how to use the Personal Year Cycle to forecast, troubleshoot, and validate your feelings and experiences as you go along.

Using the Personal Year Cycle to forecast the highest and best use of your talents and energy during the year is invaluable. Let's say last year I was in a 6 Personal Year. The basic energies of a 6 Personal Year have to do with relationships. It's the "marriage and divorce" year, where you're handed opportunities to evaluate your relationships across the board: intimate relationships, business relationships, and family relationships. It's a year where you'll be called upon to be more nurturing than usual. You'll also have a ton of personal magnetism during this year, which can be quite useful for expanding a business or attracting a mate.

True to form, last year my daughter got married, both requiring and allowing me to be a nurturing presence in the planning and execution of the festivities. I took on a lot of additional responsibility. In my professional life, I was involved in developing a new food product and also at the beginning stages of writing this book. It was a year where many of my experiences put me in the position of having to evaluate my relationships with almost everyone in my life—not in a bad way, just in an important way. Many people close to me were experiencing health concerns that required

232

some additional care and attention from me. That alone forced me to reevaluate my personal feelings about life, death, what's really important, and what I do and don't want in my life.

All in all, there was a concentration of the key elements of the number 6: nurturing of self and others, responsibility, evaluation of relationships, "marriage or divorce," a love of beauty, and embracing the bigger picture. I was able to anchor myself throughout the year, knowing that I needed to throw myself wholeheartedly into activities where these key characteristics were required of me. I was also aware of the push and pull of the challenging aspects of the 6 vibration and kept those tendencies in mind, so when I felt myself leaning toward the "dark side" of the 6 vibration I could evaluate my behavior and quickly shift toward more optimal aspects.

Knowing that I was in my 6 Personal Year was something I kept coming back to again and again when I felt a little shaky. It fortified me to embrace the key energies that the 6 vibration brought to my life. Rather than being confused or angry about the additional responsibility and feeling pressured, I innately understood that was the *purpose* of the year! At the beginning of the year, I was able to forecast based on what I expected from the 6 Personal Year. I knew up front that my daughter's wedding would be a focal point of the year and so I was able to use the information my Personal Year energies brought to me in a way I found beneficial. This was a great way to help me anticipate what would be expected of me and gave me time to think about how to establish my personal boundaries and use the positive elements of that 6 energy to my benefit.

Knowing my Personal Year Number cleared the mental clutter I might have otherwise resorted to: You know, constant mental chatter that I should be doing something else other than what I was doing. Knowing my Personal Year Cycles has given me permission to see the overarching "theme" for the year and return to that theme for guidance and validation.

Using your Personal Year Cycle can help you troubleshoot situations that come up throughout the year. Kate, a client of mine, transitioned into her 8 Personal Year this year. She's ecstatic about the changes she's experiencing and her knowledge that this year is all about money and expanding her personal power and influence has made her experiences feel on target and meaningful.

Knowing the energy for her year relates to "money and power," she's laser-beamed her intentions for making money and it's already working. Kate's getting calls to teach high-cost seminars in exciting cities. She's expanding her practice and bringing in new clients. She's written a list of several things she wants this year that will cost extra money, so she's putting it out there as her "wish list," and so far the money is rolling in. Kate trusts that with the support of the energy of her 8 Personal Year she'll be unstoppable, as long as she's focused and accepts the abundance as it flows to her.

Knowing she's in her 8 Personal Year is allowing Kate to troubleshoot as she goes along. While Kate's primarily concentrating her efforts on the optimal energies related to an 8 Personal Year, she's also well aware of the challenges and tendencies that are related to that energy. She's sufficiently familiar with her numerology to know that this is a year where money could be lost as well as gained. It's a year where her personal power will be tested, so she's keeping her antennae perked up. This way she can work mindfully with any experiences that challenge her personal power—and it's a yearlong task.

Fortunately, Kate is aware that there will be areas to which her awareness needs to be highly attuned. Her knowledge of the stumbling blocks of the 8 Personal Year will allow her to avoid getting caught up in the muck and mire the challenging aspects of the 8 Personal Year might bring up for her.

Knowing where you are in your Personal Year Cycle can validate your feelings and experiences in ways that allow for conscious growth and learning. Isn't that worth the price of admission right there? Knowing you're in a 9 Personal Year is a valuable "heads up" that it's going to be an intense year. Fortified with this knowledge, you can expect big changes. Rather than resisting those changes, you can jump in the boat and ride the wave rather than struggling and swimming against the strong current.

If you're in your 1 Personal Year, this is the beginning of a new nine-year cycle for you, so you might be extra careful to make it count and plant the seeds you'd like to see grow rather than bumble along without much drive or initiative.

Five Personal Years are always non-stop rollercoaster rides. Wouldn't it be great to plan travel and other activities related to the key energy of the number 5, like adventure, freedom, sensuality, and all that goes with it?

Heading into your 7 Personal Year? Knowing this year is perfect for reflection, for spiritual growth and learning, and for evaluation will allow you to take time for these activities rather than shoving them aside. When you realize the energy of the year supports these activities, you'll be likely to feel more in sync with yourself.

For instance, when you're in your 4 Personal Year, you know it's all about hard work and laying a foundation so you can move forward successfully in your life—all done with steady and stable steps toward your goals. Oh, and if you're in your 4 Personal Year, you'll make it much easier on yourself if you start out by clearly defining your goals.

If *developing stability and process* is your optimal baseline for measuring your activities for the 4 Personal Year, come back to that idea as you make both major and minor decisions. You can ask yourself: "Is partying late into the night and coming into work late in line with the energy of my Personal Year?" If you're in your

4 Personal Year, absolutely not. You can be sure that if you spend your year slacking off you're not developing the foundation you need to make the rest of your cycle an optimal experience for you.

Yet if you ask yourself: "Is researching a new industry that I'm interested in securing a new job, finding contacts in the field, revising my resume, and applying for the job in line with the energy of my 4 Personal Year?" then the answer is probably *yes*. The trick will be to understand the key elements of the number 4, which requires steady, practical steps toward what you're planning to accomplish. As long as you know you can't skip steps if you want to improve your success ratio.

You know what else? Knowing what Personal Year your friends and family are in the midst of is a powerful tool for developing a deeper awareness of them and understanding their lives. I find that knowing where my friends and family are in their own Personal Year Cycles allows me to key in to the core issues they're experiencing so that I can support them the best way I can. It helps me communicate with them in a richer way. In fact, I have a habit of checking the Personal Year Numbers of my close circle of friends and family at the start of each year.

This year, for example, is going to be intense for many people in my life, so—by extension—I can expect to experience intensity because of our involvement. I might not currently be in a 9 Personal Year, but several of my close family members are in theirs.

Knowing the energy surrounding your friends and family during each year is a handy tool to see what's at play with them in both their professional and personal lives. The bonus reward you reap is the potential of forging deeper understanding between you and your loved ones. Whereas in the past you may have felt you just "didn't get" why your wife did this, your father did that, or your best friend was a mess, now you will have the opportunity to step back and evaluate. See what energies their Personal Years are bringing to them so that you'll be better able to support them with their struggles and engage with them joyfully in sharing the good stuff.

Knowing the cycles of the people closest to you in your life not only can help you understand them better, it also can help *you* ready yourself for how they'll impact your life during the year.

Being Aware of Your Life Stages and Challenges

YOUR LIFE STAGES AND CHALLENGES are the last tools in your life redesign toolbox. If you go back and look at the results of your calculation of your Life Stages and Challenges, keeping those numbers handy or embedded lightly in your mind can also serve to steer you toward your optimal future and assist you in coming to terms with your past.

I'll use myself as an example in hopes that you can find the same sense of peace and clarity that I did when I applied my Life Stages and Challenges to my past and then used them as a blueprint to project into—and plan—my future.

My birth date is July 22, 1963. I'm a 3 Life Path. When I calculate my Life Stages and Challenges, here's what I get. A reminder: the first number is the Life Stage Number. The year inside the hatch marks < > is the Challenge number for that stage.

- First Stage (0–33 years):   11/2 <3>
- Second Stage (33–42 years):   5 <3>
- Third Stage (42–51 years):   7 <0>
- Fourth Stage (51 and beyond):   8 <6>

In architecture, a draftsperson works with transparent paper called a "bum wad," which is a tracing paper that allows the designer to sketch something and then overlay it on the blueprint in order to try out a different perspective or experiment with other design options without having to redo the entire blueprint every time. As you refine your blueprint for your life redesign project, this will be an overlay to your understanding of where you've been and where you're going.

This is a concept you can apply to your own blueprint for transformation. Investigating your Life Stages and Challenges is like putting a piece of bum wad over your life. When I look at my own, here's the way it serves me in striving to create my optimal self. Follow along with your own chart and see how you feel about your own Stages and Challenges.

My First Life Stage immersed me in the hyper-sensitivity of the 11/2 Master Number. Knowing this alone has allowed me a profound sense of healing. I was an extremely emotionally sensitive kid and adult, right up to that turning point of age thirty-three. Knowing the energies related to the number 11/2 and seeing that I was "swimming" in those energies for my first thirty-three years has honestly allowed me to come to a deep understanding about how I handled myself during those years.

The energy of the 11/2 is high-frequency and brings with it a certain level of nervous energy. It's a creative energy sitting on top of the 2, which is all about harmony, balance, being of service, and devotion to group dynamics. It's also all about love: specifically, the giving and receiving of unconditional love.

As a child, I was an emotional sponge, soaking in the moods of everyone around me. I became the "pleaser" in order to maintain what I felt was a more harmonious atmosphere. Especially at home, where my parents were having difficulties, I resorted to doing my "child's best" to maintain harmony in an inhospitable environment.

While some children would handle the situation much differently—perhaps by acting out or ignoring it altogether—I found that I wanted everything and everyone to be all right at all costs. Of course this was just my perception. Yet it was quite a powerful force in how I continued to construct my life from beginning early on as a pleaser who was often emotionally overwhelmed. I couldn't remember a time as a child or a young adult that I didn't feel a constant nagging sense of anxiety.

When I learned about my First Life Stage and the components of the 11/2 vibration, this information resonated with me and I felt a distinct sense of freedom from the pain I associated with some of my choices during that long period of my life.

Add to the mix that my Challenge vibration was a 3, my own Life Path Number! Really? The intensity of those years made more sense to me when I placed them in the context of the influences my numbers were dealing me. No wonder I felt emotionally fragile during those years. I was being challenged in all directions to grow into a person who is emotionally self-expressive in the highest form. No wonder it had been hard.

Then I began to clearly see the ways in which I defaulted into the destructive elements of the numbers. I struggled consistently with emotional ups and downs, with an inability to communicate clearly and authentically, with depression, and with debilitating self-doubt. Pinpointing the actual words used to describe the tendencies of the numbers I was working with was like a light bulb going off in my head. Once I could name it, I could do something about it.

Knowing this information and allowing myself to go back through past events in my mind with a new perspective on my actions gave me permission to forgive myself and see how all of it ultimately worked as a tool for my own growth, no matter how difficult it was to experience. It allowed me to open up my mind and see other key players in my life in a new way. I found myself reevaluating certain events in my life and being less hard on the people who were a part of those emotional memories. The personal freedom gained by forgiveness was invaluable.

My Second Life Stage commenced when I was thirty-three years old. This segment of my life was undeniably the most tumultuous. During this time, the 5 energy was surrounding me and I could really feel it. I felt edgy, like I had to break free and change things up in a big way.

This Life Stage was one huge freak out. My mother died from cancer, I finished my dissertation and defended it successfully. I got my doctoral degree. My marriage was unraveling. And then what? I had no idea. This was a time of deep grief for me as I attempted to deal with my mother's death. I felt lost and in despair about my own direction in life.

Then the double whammy: a 3 Challenge *again*. I'm thinking if I don't learn and exemplify the 3 energy during my lifetime I'll have missed my calling! Seeing that the key aspects of creative self-expression and communication inherent in the 3 were both my top goals and my challenges—at least for the first forty-two years of my life—was a great eye-opener for me. Even if I didn't understand it from the get go, I can now mark the turning points in my life based on the intense desire to master these skills and I can mark events when I wasn't yet strong enough to meet the challenges successfully.

Those painful times jumpstarted my progress in embodying the optimal elements of the 3 vibration. I say so because, honestly, the excruciating experiences taught me the most. Luckily, I was able to learn from the experiences rather than allow them to grind me to a pulp—even though I surely looked and felt like a pile of pulp when I was going through it.

My Third Life Stage began the year I got a divorce, a huge

transition for me. This Life Stage has since been guided by the internal exploration inherent to the 7 vibration. It's been a remarkable time for my own personal and professional growth, filled with lots of learning both in traditional classes and also in the school of practical experience.

Seeing that I'm experiencing a 0 Challenge has encouraged me make the most out of this segment of my life. With the 0 Challenge, it can go either way for me, as it's the "all or nothing" Challenge Number. Yet my understanding of numerology encourages me to believe that if I can have an awareness of, and act upon the most positive aspects of all the numbers, then I'm stepping up to my task. To me, simply having an awareness of the most positive attributes of all nine numbers provides me with substantial fuel to push me to be mindful about how I go about living my life. I'm able to think big about my goals rather than settling for "just average."

So far, knowing my Life Stages and Challenges has given me a reflective surface from which to view my life thus far. I'm in the final years of my Third Life Stage and can focus on making the best choices based on the supportive energies surrounding me for the next few years. Now I have a chance to look at my future and begin to devise my own personal blueprint for change based on what I can see before me.

My Fourth Life Stage (the final one) will begin when I'm fifty-one. It's guided by the energy of the number 8: achievement, money, power, authority. My challenge is the vibration of the 6. What's so vital about knowing this information is this: my habits and tendencies lay most squarely in the attributes of the 6. I'm in my comfort zone when I'm being nurturing, responsible, caring for others—all traits of the 6 vibration. Yet in my last Life Stage I'm being called to embark on a journey that requires that I leap into the arena of achievement and financial abundance in ways I haven't before. I can intuitively feel this, yet it's certainly pushing me out of my comfort zone.

I also feel a strong inclination toward acting on the overactive aspects of the number 6, which is why I feel it's my special challenge for this final portion of my life. It's a test for me to master and balance the best aspects of power, abundance, authority and nurturing, and responsibility while seeing the bigger picture.

Remember: Your Challenges bombard—or tempt—you with the destructive aspects of the vibration while simultaneously challenging you to *become* the optimal of the vibration. So really, you can see your Life Stages and Challenges as the Push-Me-Pull-You from *Dr. Doolittle*. Remember that animal? It looked like a llama, but with a head at either end of its body pointing in two different directions. The Life Stages and Challenges are both part of one animal, and their task is to work in tandem with each other despite the inherent difficulties in achieving harmony. It's not an impossible task, just a constant negotiation.

What this information offers me is a good look at where I'm heading and what my obstacles will be. Realizing that I'm working with the achievement-oriented 8 energy for the last stage of my life is allowing me to come to terms with the idea that a laconic retirement is most likely not in my future. It's helping me think big about my future and embrace the idea that, if I'm working optimally, I'm meant to use the skills and talents of creative expression and communication that I've been mastering as a 3 Life Path to inspire and uplift others.

When I'm doing that consistently and then tagging that into the energy of the 8, chances are in my favor to expand my financial abundance and make a difference in my own life and in the lives of others. Ultimately, that would make me happy—happy, satisfied, and content that I've lived a purposeful life, no matter how many road blocks I've encountered along the way.

Don't get me wrong, I'm not an enlightened Zen master. Far from it. I bump up against my challenges and tendencies all the time. Yet now I recognize them as my emotional "barbells:" The more I work out with them, the stronger I become.

I know you can work with your Life Stages and Challenges in much the same manner. As you study your own Life Stages and Challenges, you have an opportunity to come to terms with, deeply understand, and potentially heal your past while illuminating your optimal future.

Using your Life Stages and Challenges can help you redecorate, remodel, or renovate your life by giving you a bird's eye view of your past, present, and potential future. If you take it a step further, you can use your knowledge to look back and see what you were working with during the earlier portions of your life in order to come to terms with both pleasant and painful memories and experiences. You can chose to reconstruct your story in a way that frees you to start building the optimal *you* with renewed vigor and better results.

Take some time to review your entire Personal Year Cycle history. See how your Personal Year Cycles have merged and meshed with your Life Stages and Challenges. You can really begin to get an engaging picture of your life; past, present, and future. Use what you learn about yourself to become even clearer about what you want out of your current redecoration, remodeling, or renovation project.

Reminder: You can get a free downloadable copy of *The Redesign Your Life Workbook* at FeliciaBender.com that has pages ready for you to fill out. No need to reinvent the wheel. Print it out and save it in a binder so you can keep the information in one spot for future reference.

CHAPTER 7

THE WILDLY OPTIMAL YOU

*"Why then 'tis none to you; for there is nothing either good or
bad, but thinking makes it so."*
—William Shakespeare, *Hamlet*

I HAD A WONDERFUL EXCHANGE with someone who was
intrigued to learn his Life Path Number and his Personal Year
Cycles. We went over the information, spending time with the
overview of his life provided by reviewing all the Personal Year
Cycles up to his current year. Then he looked at me with a quizzi-
cal squint and inquired: "So what does it *mean?*"

Ultimately, the answer to this question is the crux of the matter, isn't it? You can have the proverbial key to the Universe sitting
in the palm of your hand, yet if you don't know where the ignition
is or where the lock to be opened is located, *so what?*

You can look at the benefits of numerology in different ways. If you're a business-minded person and relate most directly to business systems, take the information provided by your Life Path, Personal Year Cycle, and Life Stages and Challenges and assemble the data much as you would construct an actual business plan. Every successful business starts with a detailed plan outlining its mission and including a positioning statement and descriptions of the company's target audience, key benefits, key strengths in the marketplace, and key challenges. The plan includes other vital aspects to the identity of the company, including an explanation of its current status in the marketplace and its projected growth. Business plans most often include a timeline with goals and benchmarks for the growth of the company.

Business plans are updated annually in order to accurately reflect the actual results of the past year and refresh or expand upon the next level of projections. Some plans express "pie in the sky" dreams. When they do, the companies they describe usually fizzle out early in the game because their management is not working from realistic as well as forward-thinking plans. Other plans fail to deliver because they're too vague and ill-defined. Yet other business plans are both focused and realistic, even presenting conservative goal projections in order to leave room for happy surprises and overshooting the goals along the way.

Can you see how the meaning you derive from your numerology can play the same significance in your life as a great business plan plays in the development of a successful company? Company = business plan. You = life redesign blueprint.

Successful companies seek support and are always seeking to expand and grow, and they are usually looking for ways to improve their product. You can take charge of your life by constructing your own redesign blueprint with the same overall intent to grow and improve. You can begin to focus your project mission statement by keeping all aspects of your Life Path Number in the forefront of your mind while allowing the optimal aspects to guide your actions.

When a company strays from its primary mission statement, the company is weakened and cannot sustain the same level of results. The same can be said for you. If you stray from the optimal purpose you've outlined in your life redesign blueprint, the less happy, satisfied, and enthused you will be. Simply said: Focus on mastering what it takes to perform most often in the optimal range of your Life Path number while remaining aware of your tendencies and obstacles.

As we've been discussing, the specific information you glean from your Life Path Number, Personal Year Cycle, and Life Stages and Challenges should be the foundation of your redesign blueprint, which will help you develop and grow personally in a mindful and meaningful way. One thing that is not open to interpretation, however, is that we need to make and follow through on specific plans if we want to experience success. A company without a focused business plan is rarely successful. The same can be said for those of us who wonder why our lives aren't giving us what we want when we haven't even defined what it *is* we really want.

A business plan is an intention put forth in writing. Your redesign blueprint likewise should be an intention put forth in writing. These documents are not written in stone. They are mutable outlines that can be, and are designed to be changed, tweaked, and expanded along the way.

If you're not a business-minded person, this might sound like mumbo-jumbo to you. In that case, relate it to whatever metaphor you connect with. Are you a creative artist? Then relate your redesign blueprint to pitching your ultimate art project to the Museum of Modern Art, The Guggenheim Museum, or any other venue that excites your imagination. Use your Numbers to create your project plan from origination to installation and beyond. Artists have to plan, too. Think about your life as your ultimate creative art project and plan accordingly.

Perhaps you're sports-minded. Then use your love of sports to come up with your template for your personal Redesign Project. Training. Team selection. Game plans. Strategy. Finding your weakness and strengths—downplaying the former while exploiting the latter. It's all the same idea. Work with a structure or metaphor that works to excite your senses, as this will sustain your interest, and inspire you to follow through on your project plan.

Glitches and Surprises

AS YOU GALVANIZE YOUR PROJECT PLAN, one of the primary benefits of maintaining a firm grasp on your numerological tools resides in your actual exposure to the *questions at hand.*

Let me explain what I mean. Have you ever gone to an online dating site and filled out one of the personal profiles that's required in order for the service to offer you potential matches?

Even if you don't want to participate in online dating, I'd highly recommend taking the time to go to one of the sites and fill out the profile. You don't actually have to submit it at the end. Yet just sitting down and making yourself answer the array of questions these profiles ask of you is a great way to start thinking about yourself within the framework of these particular questions, which are all about defining and refining your sense of *who you are and what you want.*

You might skip through life without thinking much about your exact spiritual beliefs, what you truly value, how you relate and interact, your dislikes and likes, and what makes or breaks a relationship for you. Here you have the questions laid out before you and you must define as clearly as you can the answers to "Who are you and what do you want?" It's not as easy as it might appear. And more than that, you might be surprised by some of your answers.

Hammering out the details of your redecoration, remodeling, or renovation project can serve the same function and produce similar effects in your life as filling out that dating profile. Sometimes just exposing yourself to the questions is a huge step in beginning to narrow down your focus and gain clarity about who you are and what you want. If a driving force behind you reading this book is the fact that you have no clue what you really want in your life, it's my hope that knowing your numbers has given you something tangible to work with. Perhaps it has offered you a little "Eureka!" moment that will carry you forward with your redesign project.

Something to keep in mind is this: Even if you still don't know exactly what *it* is you want to do in your life, using your numerology can guide you as you explore your options. I have found that often when you're ready to redecorate, remodel, or renovate your life, you're starting out really frustrated about where you currently find yourself. Most people feel stuck. Many of us therefore enter into our redesign projects with a sense of desperation and intensity about uncovering exactly *the thing* we should be doing with our lives.

The information in this book *can't* tell you: You're a 2 Life Path = secretary. A 5 Life Path = travel guide. A 7 Life Path = Professor of Philosophy. But it can offer you information about how to focus your energies. Your Life Path Number doesn't determine what kind of work you'll do best, but it sheds light on how you approach work and defines the qualities you would bring to any job. There aren't any limits to the ways you can create your best life.

There's a bundle of ways to create the "optimal you" based on numerological guideposts. *The trick is to focus on what you uniquely bring to the expression of your Life Path Number.*

You can look at the descriptions of all the Life Path Numbers and think: "Well, that could describe anyone." In some ways, yes, when we read the Life Path profiles there are aspects that fit all of us. For instance, you're reading the defining qualities of the 4 Life Path and one of the main elements of the path is traumatic family experiences. You think: "Everyone has issues with their childhoods. Come on!" I would say you're right. However, while it can be said that almost everyone struggles with issues related to childhood, if you're a 4 Life Path this issue is particularly pronounced in the way you create your life around the pain associated with these issues. Working through these issues will be the key to you creating your best self.

You can be fully on task as a 9 Life path whether you're a nun, a high-powered businessperson, an actor, an artist, a sanitation worker, or a homemaker. The same can be said for all the Numbers. Just because you're a 1 Life Path doesn't mean the only way you'll be stepping up to your life's mission is by being a CEO, politician, or any other role that's easily defined as a "leadership" position. There are countless ways you can fulfill the 1 Life Path mission of developing creativity and confidence in everything you do. The same is true for each Life Path.

One of the obvious factors in how we end up manifesting our optimal Life Path mission has to do with our influences. Rich opportunity comes from deciding how to use our influences to create our optimal lives. Perhaps a bigger challenge resides in how to slog through the difficult influences we've had and come out the other side in one piece.

For instance, have you ever thought of how many ways there are to learn compassion? For some, the experience of having cancer, nurturing a sibling who is handicapped, or being personally involved in military action is a conduit to learning compassion. Whereas someone else might need less shock-value and could learn compassion by the example set by a beloved grandparent, by interacting with the less fortunate, or learning early on how to care for animals. Either way, the end result has the potential to be "learning compassion."

The same can be said for you as you travel your Life Path. How many different ways are there to learn creativity and confidence when you're on the 1 Life Path?

Creating cooperation and harmony comes in many shapes when you're on the 2 Life Path.

How can you develop authentic communication and creative self-expression as a 3 Life Path?

The 4 Life Path challenges you with any manner of avenues to develop stability and process in whatever you choose to do.

Are you a 5 Life Path with an intense desire for freedom and adventure or do you have an aversion to these things? Either way, your mission is to balance freedom with discipline.

When you're on the 6 Life Path, let me count the ways you can choose to develop your mission of nurturing and acceptance.

When you're walking the 7 Life Path, be sure you'll be met with every opportunity to examine and strengthen your sense of trust and openness.

As an 8 Life Path, you'll be bombarded with every way imaginable to work on your sense of personal power and develop both material and spiritual abundance throughout your life.

Do you have a 9 Life Path? Be certain you'll be handed lots of experiences with the potential to teach you to develop integrity and wisdom in all you do.

Yet one of my promises in this book has been that knowing

your numerology will assist you in a practical way by paring down and exposing the core elements to your primary purpose in your life. So while there aren't any limits as to how to get there, the ticket for you is to continue to go back to the "spine" of who you are —defined by your Life Path Number—as you apply those key goals to the decisions you make as you redecorate, remodel, or renovate your life.

The idea is to act on who you are *right now,* knowing that you'll refine and reinvent yourself as you go along. Life is dynamic, yet you can only begin from exactly where you are at this moment. Don't beat yourself up for being in a tough spot. Don't regret the choices you made that have led you to a crisis. Instead, take responsibility for your past choices, clean up your messes (if there are messes to clean up), and commit to taking the lessons you've learned to heart and making optimal choices *now.*

Anchor yourself with your Life Path Number.

Look to your Personal Year Cycle for guidance and light structure as you determine your best route.

Check your Life Stage Numbers and Challenge Numbers to reconfigure and understand where you are, what you're working with, and where you might be headed.

As you do this with consistency, prepare yourself for glitches in your plan and work with flexibility to move with or around them. Simply tuning in to your knowledge of your Life Path and your Personal Year Cycle offers you an effective method to work with the constant glitches and surprises you're bound to experience in life. When you understand that each year carries a special energy that demands you concentrate on specific aspects of your personality, behavior, and your relationships, you're already a huge step ahead. You aren't *expecting* things to be the same or be measured with the same "ruler" year in and year out.

The 7 Essential Redesign Questions

LET'S REVISIT THE SEVEN KEY QUESTIONS you'll use as you develop your personal blueprint for redecorating, remodeling, or renovating your life.

1. What do I want to redecorate, remodel, or renovate in my life?
2. What are the main components of my Life Path mission?
3. How have my past decisions and actions, as they relate to my project, aligned or conflicted with my overarching Life Path mission?
4. How can I more closely align my decisions and actions, as they relate to my project, with my overarching Life Path mission?
5. What are my next three project-specific action items?
6. What is my time frame for accomplishing each action item?
7. How do I know when my action item is completed?

Here's one more example so you can really get this format under your belt and into your new redesign toolbox.

Rebecca is a fifty-seven-year old 3 Life Path and wants to redesign her life by changing her career path. She owns a small health club and business hasn't done as well as she'd like. She has a year left before she needs to decide to renew her lease or not, so she's thinking about what she'd truly like to do in her life and career.

Luckily, Rebecca is listening to her inner voice, because she's just a year away from her second and last Saturn Return, the point in which she's asking herself: "Now or never. Who am I and what do I want to do in the world?" During her first Saturn Return, Rebecca went through a major transition in her career. So she certainly shows consistency. And remember this about Saturn Returns: these are intense periods in your life where you'll feel an urgent need to evaluate what you're doing and make big decisions about what you want for the next phase of your life. Your Saturn Return is a tough inquisitor who's asking you if you're disciplined enough to make the big changes in your life that you need to make.

Rebecca has no issues with self-confidence regarding her academic achievements. She has a Masters in Counseling and used to work in a managed care setting. She got married and had a son during one of her number 9 Personal Years. She became dissatisfied with the corporate environment where she was working and decided to buy one small health club and then another. She manages the business aspects of the clubs and also works behind the desk. She's tired of managing the business and is feeling drawn toward something that feels more meaningful to her, although she's not exactly sure what that might be.

During her life, Rebecca has always had weight issues. When she talks about her weight, it's truly an old issue she has grappled with since childhood. As Rebecca talks about her family and upbringing, it's clear that she comes from family who doesn't encourage emotional self expression in the least. Rebecca mentions her mother and that she wishes they had a better relationship. She observes with a light laugh that it's no mystery why she is fat; she over eats. She says she finds comfort and control in her consumption of food. She's able to observe that—when confronted with uncomfortable emotions—it's her habit to either laugh it off or ignore it all together.

Reviewing Rebecca's Life Stages uncovers some great clues to her life's blueprint. From birth to age 33, Rebecca's Life Stage Number was a 3—the same vibration as her Life Path. This energy supported her in becoming a healthy communicator and a fountain of creative self-expression. Yet Rebecca's family wasn't supportive of this kind of expression. It wasn't encouraged, so Rebecca became detached and cautious about even locating the emotions that were inside her. Her Challenge Number during this First Life Stage added to her sense of helplessness. Her early life had a 1 Challenge, where she was being called upon to stand up for herself and be true to herself. Especially during a first Life Stage, this challenges confidence and also brings in people and circumstances that feel dominating.

Rebecca's Second Life Stage began at a 9 Personal Year and it was tumultuous. This was the year she became a mother. This Life Stage was guided by the Master 11/2 energy, where Rebecca was being asked to work in support of group dynamics and become a master of cooperation and harmony. She really threw herself into her new motherhood role and gave up certain aspects of her career in order to stay home and be with her son. Fittingly, her Challenge during this Second Life Stage was an 8 vibration, which (if you recall) is all about money, achievement, and personal power. She felt guilty and pulled in different directions; she wanted to be a good mother and she also felt the strong desire to continue achieving in her job. This was a challenging time for Rebecca as she attempted to balance the demands of family and work.

Rebecca's Third Life Stage started—again during a 9 Personal Year—and she felt the pressure of that demanding 9 Personal Year. She changed jobs. Her son was in school and she was able to focus again on her career. This stage was guided by a 5 energy. Everything was changing at a rapid pace and Rebecca found it exhilarating and also scary. She gained weight. She started feeling an overwhelming desire to learn new things; many subjects metaphysical in nature. Her Challenge Number during this Third Life Stage was a 7 and she appeared to grab onto the more constructive elements of her Challenge. She turned inward, reading and gaining knowledge, seeking spiritually-based information, and questioning her life in a renewed way.

Her Fourth and final Life Stage is again an 11/2 vibration with another 7 challenge. When we spoke, Rebecca commented that she would really like to get to the bottom of her weight issues after all these years. She's excited by the new spiritual weight loss books being released and thinks reading these might start her in the right direction. She mentioned that she's being pulled toward the idea of teaching in some capacity. She's understanding that a major aspect of her 3 Life Path mission is to not only come to terms with her emotional life, but also to use her hard-won authentic emotional life to help heal and inspire others.

What do I want to redecorate, remodel, or renovate in my life? Rebecca started out wanting to remodel her career, yet as she progressed, she realized that she also wanted to renovate her health by getting to the bottom of her weight problem. Notice how she didn't just want to lose fifty pounds. Rebecca really wanted to understand and come to terms with her life-long weight issues. She's definitely committing to a renovation project. Remember: often your redesign project will have intersecting issues, which makes it even more important to write down each issue separately while also working with them together when they collide with each other.

What are the main components of my Life Path Mission? Being a 3 Life Path, Rebecca chose these primary elements of her Life Path Mission to focus on: "joy, emotional self-expression, communication, light-hearted, good at lots of things, at the end of the day—my mission is to inspire and heal myself and others." She then wrote down the key challenges she feels she faces as a 3 Life Path: "self-doubt, lacking follow-through, scattered, depression."

How have my past decisions and actions, as they relate to my renovation project, aligned or conflicted with my overarching Life Path mission? As a 3 Life Path, Rebecca has mastered the intellectual aspects of her gifts. She has a master's degree and works effectively in professional situations. What she began discovering as she focused on her career and health renovation project is that she's not yet mastered her understanding of her emotions and then how to express them in a healthy way. Rebecca started realizing that she's been "eating" her emotions since childhood and she's beginning to see that the key to her weight loss is to explore these uncomfortable emotions she has been denying all these years. As she began to outline her project, she set her priority project to be "to get to the bottom of my weight issues." Her secondary project ended up being the remodeling of her career. As she prioritized her projects, she began to see how getting her weight under control could potentially segue into helping her find a solution to her career questions.

How can I more closely align my decisions and actions, as they relate to my renovation project, with my overarching Life Path mission? It was actually a shock to Rebecca to begin to see how detached she is emotionally. It look some excavating for her to admit that many of her memories about her childhood and her relationship with her parents—particularly her mother—were very painful. Only after learning about her numerology and having her Life Path information resonate with her could Rebecca begin to see how important her emotional life is to leading the life she's longing for. Before, she was able to retreat into her academic performance, her professional performance, and food. Yet now, she's finding that isn't satisfying to her and she wants to feel more authentic and more emotionally involved in her own life. Before knowing the basics of her 3 Life Path mission, Rebecca was able to avoid identifying the way she truly feels. With her Life Path information in her toolbox, Rebecca is finding more courage to delve into exploring her emotional life, past and present.

What are my next three project-specific action items? Rebecca decided on these three action items to start out her project.

1. Rebecca started meditating several years ago. She was willing to do this meditation as her first action item: *Give your heavy self a name. Give your healthy-weight self a name. In a meditative state, start a conversation with your heavy self. Get to know her. She really is your friend and protector. She's in your life for a reason. Ask her why she's there. Then ask her what it would take for her to retire? Have the same conversation with your thin self, only ask her why she's hiding? Ask her why she doesn't show up very often? Conclude your meditation by embracing what both aspects—thin and heavy—have to teach you about yourself.*

2. As a 3 Life Path, Rebecca decided she was taking life much too seriously. In order for her to get in touch with her emotional life, Rebecca realized she needed to *lighten up*, both literally and figuratively. Her second action item is to take a class in something she's interested in learning about that would offer her a chance to explore something that might make her happy and help her begin to lose weight, like a dance class, a fun new exercise class, or cooking class geared toward light, healthier recipes.

3. Rebecca's final action item was to finish reading the new spiritual weight-loss book that she hadn't had time to read.

What is my time frame for accomplishing each action item? #1: Rebecca gave herself one week to do this thirty-minute meditation three times; #2: two weeks to find a class she was excited about taking and signing up during that time period; #3: realistically, she wanted to finish the book in one week but knew her husband had planned an outing for that weekend and so she gave herself permission to extend her deadline for reading the book to two weeks.

How do I know when my action item is completed? Often, this is easy. Other times, a bit more difficult to gauge. For Rebecca, she can certainly check off her first three action items in a fairly concrete manner: did the meditation, signed up and started the class, finished the book. Yet when she's done with the first three action items, then it's time to add the next three until she meets the goal she sets up for herself. So an action item that might be more difficult to determine a conclusion to might be: "To start asking my mother questions about my childhood." This can be an ongoing action item that becomes a part of the "optimal you" that you're developing. You can check this action item off your list when conversation about your childhood with your mother becomes a "normal" part of your relationship together. You've then achieved the ultimate renovation for yourself and for your ongoing goal of becoming connected with your authentic emotions.

An end note to Rebecca's renovation project: Rebecca decided that a great step for her was to start a weight loss book club at the health club she owns. She posted the meetings on her bulletin board and sent out email invitations to all the members of her club. She was able to see if she really enjoyed teaching (something she'd been drawn to as a 3 Life Path) by leading the book club.

She found strength in relaying her experiences with other men and women who struggle with their weight for similar reasons.

By aligning herself with the optimal elements of her 3 Life Path—which for Rebecca included getting up in front of an audience and teaching while inspiring and uplifting others—she was energized by feeling much more on track in her life. Even though there were aspects to starting to lead a group that made her uncomfortable, leading the book club provided Rebecca with a sense of direction she'd been longing to experience. She started her project with this thought: "I want to do something more meaningful with my life." By going through the Seven Essential Redesign Questions and following the Rule of Three, Rebecca was able to find more clarity about what direction she wanted to take both her career and her health.

Fail Forward

ONE OF THE INEVITABLE RESULTS as you seek to redecorate, remodel, or renovate your life is failure. Yes, the "F" word. Do you usually consider yourself a success or a failure? And how do you qualify that label? Are you a "success" at your job yet a "failure" at your relationships? Or vice versa? Or do you simply have snippets of experiences seared into your mind when you felt highly successful or a dismal failure? What does it really mean and how does it affect you now?

Scott Adams, the creator of the cartoon *Dilbert,* wrote an engaging article in the *Wall Street Journal* titled "How to Get a Real Education" (April 9, 2011). Among other intriguing points of view about education and entrepreneurship, Adams makes several suggestions: 1) Combine skills and make yourself valuable; 2) fail forward, if you're really taking risks you should find yourself failing 90 percent of the time; 3) attract luck; and 4) conquer fear and replace it with enthusiasm.

I find that people get wrapped up with this "failure python" until it literally squeezes the life out of them. People view not having succeeded in doing something as an embarrassing humiliation that is something to be avoided at all costs. What if we shifted our thoughts and expectations to include failure as simply another type of life experience?

Former thought: "I'm divorced, so I have a failed marriage."

New thought: "I'm divorced. I had a successful marriage that has now ended."

Wouldn't that shift in thinking be a kick in the pants? To actually see and appreciate what you gleaned out of the experience so you could use that knowledge in an empowering way as you continue to create your life?

I love Adams' observation when he says: "The trick is to get paid while you're doing the failing and to use the experience to gain skills that will be useful later. I failed at my first career in banking. I failed at my second career with the phone company. But you'd be surprised at how many of the skills I learned in those careers can be applied to almost any field, including cartooning." Then he makes a very important point: *"[People] should be taught that failure is a process, not an obstacle."*

Isn't that rather mind-blowing to consider? How would our lives be different if we were told from birth onward that failure isn't to be avoided? Quite the contrary: It should be relished . . . Chewed up and spit out . . . Dissected and analyzed . . . Embraced as a conduit to ultimate success when processed and applied to new thoughts and new activities. If we fully understood and realized that failure is indeed a process, our anxiety levels and the fear factor in our lives would certainly be reduced. And instead of giving up on our dreams, our failures would renew our passion, helping us focus on revising and revitalizing our dreams until they become reality.

Tweaking, Expanding, Changing

I ADMIRE THE SHAKESPEARE QUOTE from *Hamlet*: "Why then 'tis none to you; for there is nothing either good or bad, but thinking makes it so." As you work through your redesign process, I trust you can begin to put this idea into action. We're human, so of course we can't achieve this 100 percent of the time. Perhaps if we can achieve this 51 percent of the time we're leaning in the right direction. If we can begin to see the ways that we continue to experience the obstacles and display certain tendencies outlined by our Life Path Numbers, perhaps we can come to terms with some of the thoughts and perceptions that are holding us back from creating our optimal lives.

How many people do you know who base their lives on snapshots of moments they've collected in their minds? The family member who won't speak with Uncle Ed because of something he said or did ten years ago? Your friend who won't allow herself to have a truly intimate relationship because of her short-lived marriage to an alcoholic? The child who remembers his dad telling him that he's a "quitter," so now he is?

What tapes do you replay in your own head that have defined your choices in your life and ultimately created the life you're currently leading?

This isn't to say that maybe you don't like Uncle Ed and would rather not be around him. Surely your marriage to the alcoholic has provided you with some terrific examples of what you do and don't want in an intimate relationship. If you became a quitter because your father's words had such a powerful effect on you, can you now see a way to not take his words personally and instead see how the same words may have been based in his own fears, regrets, or other issues?

Knowing your own numerology and the numerology of those close to you has the potential to help you step back and see that everyone in your life is living their own Life Path experience. You may be a part of it, but certainly you're not *it*. This may sound rudimentary, yet these are core issues that come up over and over again with clients as they set up their redesign project. Especially the parent/child relationship is a wonderful place to start using your tools. What was your father dealing with in his own life? What is his life mission as defined by his Life Path Number? Where was he in his Personal Year Cycle when he started having a family?

What's your mother's Life Path Number? Does your knowledge of her life mission shed any light on your relationship? Can you see how she may have been struggling and where she was on target with her life path mission? We have a tendency to think only of ourselves and our own needs when we reflect on our childhoods. I challenge you to explore the dynamics your parents might have been experiencing as you were growing up. I believe your numerological window will offer you a different perspective on your very human parents.

I'm not suggesting that everyone has had a traumatic childhood. Some people absolutely have had supportive and happy childhoods. That's a wonderful thing. If you're one of these fortunate folks, you'll still gain insight into your family dynamics if you apply your knowledge of the Life Path Numbers and Personal Year Cycle to your family members.

Oftentimes, when you start living within your own sense of

REDESIGN YOUR LIFE

authenticity and creativity, you end up with a life you could never even have fathomed possible. I want to stress the concept that your redesign blueprint is just that: a blueprint. It's a thought-out plan that is always ready for tweaking as you start working on it. I know very few homes that are built exactly as the original architect's blueprint prescribes. A blueprint is a sound and solid base, yet as you begin construction, you'll actually be involved in the real space—not in your mind or on a piece of paper.

Only in practice can you get a true vision of how a home design feels: if this is the right color choice, if that wall needs to be bumped out just a few more inches. The same is true in life design. In practice, as you apply the Rule of Three to taking multiple actions steps one after the other, you'll gain more clarity about what you want and how to achieve your goals, how to grow as a person and improve your relationships and the way you go about doing things. The key is to be prepared with your tools and get as skilled as possible at using them. Then you can change things with confidence and trust your intuition when things feel off or need a slightly different angle.

Personally, I am living a life now that I never even dreamed about. I set out with certain intentions based on the optimal elements of my own Life Path Number. I'm committed to living a mindful life. And now I look around and I'm doing things I could not have imagined, yet here it is. My outcome has surpassed my original intentions. Yet I had to be open to certain detours along the way. I've had to let go of certain expectations and adjust to new ones.

This is why I want to remind you that there will be surprises and glitches along the way and that these aren't always negative. I want to stress the idea that sometimes when things don't turn out the way you want them to, there's a reason. That reason usually involves pushing and challenging you in your personal evolution.

264

Perhaps losing your job threw you into depression and you allowed it to take you down into a deep, dark place for quite a while. But perhaps losing your job is the best thing that ever happened to you: You grieved the loss and then set up your new job intentions in alignment with the key components of your Life Path Number.

Even with the cry of the "poor economy," I know people who scored the job of their dreams by looking forward with a sense of expansion and—yes—optimism. They chose positions that are more in line with their essential Life Path mission, however they define it. No one wants to hire a depressed or cynical person. So if you can glean a sense of strength and purpose from your Numbers, you might find that your next position is much more suitable to your Life Path mission. Success stories usually come from people willing to step outside of their own boxes.

There have been many times when I've felt an acute sense of urgency and despair about the need to change my life. Have you felt this way? Being familiar with numerology has given me the opportunity to embrace an important concept: You're not sup-posed to be "fixed" when you work through your numerology. (Actually, nothing you learn will ever *fix* you.)

I know people who are psychic junkies, waiting for a reading that'll explain to them *exactly* what they're supposed to be doing with their lives. Some people dive into a certain diet thinking it will fix all their problems. Some follow a certain spiritual teacher in hopes that they'll be enlightened with *the answer*. You might have a desire for numerology to do the same thing for you. It won't.

What it will do—just like a good psychic reading, following a reasonable diet, or enhancing your spirituality—is provide plenty of information for you to sift through, ponder, practice, test, and use for your growth and expansion throughout your life. I'm a keen believer in the idea that if something catches you—*when it resonates deeply with you*—you should dive in. The same goes for the three tools in Part Two, "The Numerology Toolbox." Add these to your collection. Use numerology by itself or in tandem with some of your other favorite tools for the best results.

Say you're a 2 Life Path and have spent all of your life ruminating about why other people hurt your feelings all the time and this sense of hurt has controlled your life in a negative way. You've gone to counseling, yet you still can't figure out why this happens to you. If you then learn about your Life Path Number, its optimal qualities and tendencies, and the obstacles you'll be most prone to experience, there's potential for you to cut to the chase and really get to the bottom of your issues in a way that more generalized solutions don't provide. When you begin to base your decisions in your life on your optimal Life Path mission, you will attract the opportunities for growth that will lead you in the direction you want to go.

You're a 4 Life Path and all you want is a home that is your peaceful sanctuary, and yet everything you're doing takes you away from this one simple goal. You're lost in confusion, exhaustion, and frustrated because you keep rambling around and making half-baked choices about your living arrangements. Now you've learned your Life Path mission is about developing stability and process. Establishing a stable home is a big thing for you in order to establish your sense of security. No wonder why this is an issue that's at the top of your list.

With someone else, this would seem silly. "What's your problem? Just find a place and move in!" your friends keep telling you. But since this is a key element in your Life Path mission, it'll be something that's a big deal and also a big challenge for you in your life. If you know that, you can tune in to it in a different way. Knowing this is a key issue for your happiness and success might give you the additional fuel to get off your tush and make some empowering decisions regarding your living arrangements. Rather than floundering around in a pool of paralyzing confusion, being able to pinpoint the issue and some possible solutions to it can save you a whole heap of time, energy, and unhappiness.

This is only one example of how you can use your new tools of numerology to get to the crux of the matter as opposed to circling around it for years. You'll still be required to make potentially difficult decisions, take concerted action, and work through the challenges with fortitude and tenacity. Yet this tool can certainly help you narrow down the playing field so that it feels more manageable.

When you're clear about how to go about thinking about the change you want from your redecoration, remodel, or renovation project, the more likely it is that you'll surpass even your highest expectations. Tools of numerology offer you a fast track to defining core issues and how to best go about working with them. Then it's up to you to follow through with focused action, gaining valuable skill using your best tools rather than letting them collect dust in your toolbox.

Now is the time to move forward on your redesign project, no matter how big or how small it is. I hope you're feeling jazzed about putting this new information into action. I trust you've been able to go through your own numbers and ask yourself some of the key questions you'll need to break through some of your persistent barriers and make some real change in your life.

As you begin to anchor yourself to the optimal elements of your Life Path mission, you'll start feeling the difference as you make more and more choices that are in alignment with your Life Path talents. As I've stressed often throughout this book, it's all a lifelong exploration. If you're able to put your new numerological tools to use in your daily life, you'll offer yourself a new sense of clarity about your decision-making.

I know that my life has been enriched with my knowledge of

numerology. It's become a valuable tool in my own toolbox as I work to construct my most purposeful and passionate life. I hope you get some of the same "zings" that I've gotten, which I've seen other people get, when they feel a connection with what their Numbers mean for them. Then the real question comes in. They ask: "Can I actually use this information to change my life in a tangible way?" I trust that *Redesign Your Life* has provided you with a contemporary way to use the ancient art and science of numerology to help you construct the optimal you in a very real and practical way.

I hope you find the prospect of diving into your project energizing rather than daunting, and that you've developed a sense of validation about your identity and character and who you'd like to become. Ultimately, that's what it's all about. Enjoy yourself as you redesign your life.

RECOMMENDED RESOURCES

Numerology

THERE ARE A PLETHORA of books devoted to the art and science of numerology. Here are some of the books I used as the resource material for *Redesign Your Life*. I extrapolated the core of the definitions of the Life Path numbers, the Personal Year Cycles, and the Life Stages and Challenges from the following sources:

Brill, Michael. *Numerology for Decoding Behavior: Your Personal Numbers at Work, with Family, and in Relationships* (Destiny Books, Rochester, Vermont and Toronto, Canada: 2011). awakener.com

Brill, Michael. *Numerology for Healing: Your Personal Numbers as the Key to a Healthier Life* (Destiny Books, Rochester, Vermont: 2009). awakener.com

Decoz, Hans. *Numerology: Key To Your Inner Self* (A Perigee Book, the Penguin Group, New York: 1994). Decoz.com

Frederick, Sue. *I See Your Dream Job: A Career Intuitive Shows You How to Discover What You Were Put on Earth to Do* (St. Martin's Press, New York: 2009). Careerintuitive.org

Javane, Faith. *Master Numbers: Cycles of Divine Order* (Whilford Press, Atglen, PA: 1988).

Kirkman, Patricia and Katherine A. Gleason. *The Complete Idiot's Guide: Numerology Workbook* (Alpha Books, the Penguin Group, New York: 2004) patriciakirkman.com and katherine-gleason.com

Lagerquist, Kay Ph.D and Lisa Lenard. *The Complete Idiot's Guide to Numerology: Release the power of spiritual numerology in your life* (Alpha Books, the Penguin Group, New York: 2009). numerology-insights.com

Line, Julia. *The Numerology Workbook: Understanding and Using the Power of Numbers* (Sterling Publishing Co., Inc., New York: 1985).

McCants, Glynis. *Glynis Has Your Number: Discover What Life Has in Store for You Though the Power of Numerology* (Hyperion, New York: 2005). Numberslady.com

McCants, Glynis. *Love by the Numbers: How to Find Great Love or Reignite the Love You Have Through the Power of Numerology* (Sourcebooks Casablanca, Naperville, IL: 2009). Numberslady.com

Millman, Dan. *The Life You Were Born To Live: A Guide To Finding Your Life Purpose* (New World Library, 1993). Peacefulwarrior.com

Oken, Alan. *Numerology Demystified* (The Crossing Press, Freedom, CA: 1996). Alanoken.com

Phillips, David A. *The Complete Book of Numerology:*

Discovering the Inner Self (Hay House, Inc., 1992).

Strayhorn, Lloyd. *Numbers and You: A Numerology Guide for Everyday Living* (Ballantine Books, New York: 1997).

Astrology

THE ASTROLOGICAL CONCEPT of the Saturn Return is mentioned in Sue Frederick's *I See Your Dream Job*. More information is available about this transit in Schostak and Weiss's book as well as in other books focused on astrology. Jan Spiller's book is a nice companion to many of the concepts presented in *Redesign Your Life*.

Schostak, Sherene and Stefanie Iris Weiss. *Surviving Saturn's Return: Overcoming the Most Tumultuous Time In Your Life* (McGraw-Hill, New York: 2004).

Spiller, Jan. *Astrology for the Soul* (Bantam Books, New York: 1997). Janspiller.com

Perception and Thinking

I DISCUSS MANY AVENUES that might assist in altering a sense of perception about how you think about your life. The following books are a small selection of valuable reading if you desire to know more about how to achieve a shift in thinking.

Hicks, Esther and Jerry Hicks "The Teachings of Abraham." *The Amazing Power of Deliberate Intent: Living the Art of Allowing* (Hay House: 2006). abraham-hicks.com

Hicks, Esther and Jerry Hicks "The Teachings of Abraham."

Ask and It Is Given: Learning to Manifest Your Desires (Hay House: 2004). abraham-hicks.com

Hicks, Esther and Jerry Hicks "The Teachings of Abraham." *Money, and the Law of Attraction: Learning to Attracting Wealth, Health, and Happiness* (Hay House: 2008). abraham-hicks.com

Katie, Byron and Stephen Mitchell. *Loving What Is: Four Questions That Can Change Your Life* (Three Rivers Press, a division of Crown Publishing Group, New York: 2002). Thework.com

Katie, Byron and Michael Katz. *I Need Your Love - Is That True? How to Stop Seeking Love, Approval, and Appreciation and Start Finding Them Instead* (Three Rivers Press, a division of Crown Publishing Group, New York: 2005). Thework.com

Ruiz, Don Miguel. *The Four Agreements: A Practical Guide to Personal Freedom* (Amber-Allen Publishing: 1997). Miguelruiz. com

Intuition and Healing

WHEN YOU BEGIN TO REDESIGN you life, you might have questions about health and healing. I have found these resources to be a great place to start exploring the link between emotions, energy, and healing.

Co, Master Stephen and Eric B. Robins, M.D. (with John Merryman) *Your Hands Can Heal Your: Pranic Healing Energy Remedies to Boost Vitality and Speed Recovery from Common Health Problems* (The Free Press, New York: 2002). Yourhandscanhealyou. com

Myss, Caroline, Ph.D. *Why People Don't Heal and How They Can* (Harmony Books, New York: 1997). Myss.com

Schulz, Dr. Mona Lisa. *Awakening Intuition: Using Your Mind-Body Network for Insight and Healing* (Harmony Books, New York: 1998). drmonalisa.com

Sui, Choa Kok. *Pranic Healing* (Samuel Weisner, Inc., York Beach, Maine, 1990). Pranichealing.com

Life Strategy

THERE ARE SO MANY RESOURCES about how to live your best and most passionate life. Here is a "short-list" of starters for you.

Attwood, Janet Bray and Chris Attwood. *The Passion Test: The Effortless Path to Finding Your Life Purpose* (Plume/The Penguin Group, New York: 2008). Janetattwood.com

Fields, Jonathan. *Uncertainty: Turning Fear and Doubt into Fuel for Brilliance* (Penguin Group, New York: 2011). Jonathanfields. com

Rath, Tom. *Strengths Finder 2.0* (Gallup Press, New York: 2007). Strengthsfinder.com

Sher, Barbara with Barbara Smith. *I Could Do Anything If I Only Knew What It Was: How to discover what you really want and how to get it* (Dell Publishing, New York: 1994). Barbarasher.com

ACKNOWLEDGMENTS

GRATITUDE TO STEPHANIE GUNNING, extraordinary editor, expert writer, coach, teacher, and friend.

Bob VonEschen, my daily inspiration and example of the law of attraction in action.

Thank you the Book Designers for a wonderful design experience.

Thank you to Sue Frederick for your wisdom and support. You make a big difference in the lives of so many people.

Gratitude to the core of my support system, who've offered their time, energy, and expertise in test-reading this manuscript and generally being great cheerleaders: Lori Barsky, Miranda Bender, Phoebe Bender, Sandi Bianchi, Cat Cantor, Ruth Ann Hensley, Jody Howard, Jodi Jinks, Kay Alton Jones, Amy Mayer, Donna Minard, Melanie Morgan, Sharon Neathery, Linda Nehls, Andrea Nichols, Candace Nolan, and Jan Squier.

ABOUT THE AUTHOR

FELICIA BENDER, Ph.D. facilitates her "Redesign Your Life" process with individual clients and groups. She spent many years as a wife and mother before earning advanced degrees in theatre from the University of Missouri-Columbia. She's a certified Pranic Healing® practitioner, life strategist, and real estate agent. Felicia's currently involved as an investor and developer of a new food product, Snack Adventures. She lives in Boulder, Colorado.